D1060191

COLLECTIVISM

A FALSE UTOPIA

THE MACMILLAN COMPANY
NEW YORK · BOSTON · CHICAGO · DALLAS
ATLANTA · SAN FRANCISCO

MACMILLAN & CO., LIMITED
LONDON · BOMBAY · CALCUTTA
MELBOURNE

THE MACMILLAN COMPANY
OF CANADA, LIMITED
TORONTO

COLLECTIVISM
A FALSE UTOPIA

BY

WILLIAM HENRY CHAMBERLIN

NEW YORK
THE MACMILLAN COMPANY
1937

Copyright, 1936, by
THE MACMILLAN COMPANY.

All rights reserved—no part of this book may be
reproduced in any form without permission in writing
from the publisher, except by a reviewer who wishes
to quote brief passages in connection with a review
written for inclusion in magazine or newspaper.

Set up and printed. Published April, 1937.
Reprinted August, 1937.

PRINTED IN THE UNITED STATES OF AMERICA
NORWOOD PRESS LINOTYPE, INC.
NORWOOD, MASS., U.S.A.

335
C44

Tush. $2.00

INTRODUCTION

It often happens that the absence of something is the best means of teaching a sense of its value. And the strongest positive conviction I carried away from a stay of almost twelve years in the Soviet Union was of the absolute, unconditional value of human liberty. This conviction was strengthened by a shorter period of observation of the workings of another type of collectivist dictatorship in Germany.

Largely as a result of my impressions of the Soviet Union and of Germany I came to the conclusion that the most important issue which confronts civilization in the present century is that of democracy versus dictatorship. A question that, in my opinion, far transcends in importance the precise point at which the line may be drawn between public and private enterprise in economic life, is whether the people are to own the state or whether the state is to own the people, as it very definitely does in the modern-style dictatorship. It is no exaggeration to say that the whole future of Western civilization, with its many humanist and individualist roots, is very intimately bound up with the answer which history will supply to this question.

The book attempts to set forth a reasoned case

20531

for the proposition that collectivism, both in its communist and in its fascist forms, is a false utopia, on the basis of the demonstrable facts of the Soviet, Germany, and Italian experiments. There is also an effort to show the positive complement of this negative proposition: that free institutions possess a pragmatic value far outweighing the largely illusory advantages of the short-cut methods of dictatorship.

It is impossible to write such a book without thinking with admiration and sympathy of the many conscious martyrs and the still more numerous unconscious victims of the three major post-war dictatorships, with their philosophies of class, race, and national fanaticism. One hopes that this long tale of heroism and suffering has not been in vain, and that the peoples of the countries which remain free will be strengthened in their resolution to preserve at all costs the method of liberty as they realize more clearly the moral and material and cultural price of its abandonment.

My acknowledgment and thanks are due to the editors of the "Christian Science Monitor" and to the editor of the "American Mercury," who have kindly permitted me to incorporate in the book excerpts from articles which I previously contributed to these publications.

WILLIAM HENRY CHAMBERLIN

TOKYO
November, 1936

CONTENTS

COLLECTIVISM

A FALSE UTOPIA

CHAPTER I

THE REVOLT AGAINST LIBERTY

BEFORE the World War it would have seemed banal and superfluous to make out a case for human liberty, so far as North America and the greater part of Europe were concerned. Such things as regular elections, freedom of press and speech, security against arbitrary arrest, torture, and execution, were taken for granted in almost all leading countries. People could travel freely in foreign lands without worrying overmuch about passports and were not liable to be arrested by the police of one insolvent country if they failed to declare a few bills of the currency of its equally insolvent neighbor at the border. Concentration camps for political recalcitrants and the wholesale conscription of forced labor as a means of getting public works done were unknown.

Of course there were dark spots on the European horizon, such as Tsarist Russia and the Semi-Oriental Balkans. There were individual cases in which justice and freedom were obviously denied and trampled on. Such cases, however, were exceptions to be denounced, not rules of administrative practice to be accepted as

1

normal and regular. The main trend was unmistakably in the direction of extending the area of political, personal, and civil liberty.

It is an ironical sequel to the war that was supposed to safeguard the world for democracy that today the European picture is entirely different. The history of the post-war phase in Europe has been one of severe and unbroken defeats for the ideals of democracy and individual liberty. The revolutions of the twentieth century, unlike those of the eighteenth and the nineteenth, have led to the contraction, not to the expansion, of freedom. The two main governmental philosophies which have emerged since the war, fascism and communism, are based, in practice, on the most rigid regimentation of the individual.

Before proceeding further with an analysis of the revolt against liberty it is obviously desirable to have a definition of what liberty is. Stalin, Hitler, and Mussolini, in all seriousness, have repeatedly expressed the conviction that their regimes are the freest in the world. Indeed, anyone who would audibly express a contrary opinion in the Soviet Union, Germany, or Italy would soon receive convincing proof, if not of the incorrectness of his opinion, at least of the inexpediency of voicing it, by being consigned to a jail or concentration camp.

Four indispensable foundation stones of liberty, in my opinion, are freedom of speech, press, assembly, and election. Equally important are safeguards for the individual against arbitrary arrest and against imprisonment or other punishment except after a fair and open trial, in accordance with a prescribed legal code; freedom of trade-union organization and of religious practice and profession.

Inasmuch as strange tricks and parodies have been played with most of these conceptions under the modern-style dictatorships it is necessary to define some of them more explicitly. The reality of freedom of speech, for instance, may fairly be measured by the amount of criticism of governmental measures and policies that may be uttered without risk of putting the critic in prison. Freedom of press cannot be said to exist when every newspaper is either directly under the control of the ruling party or is subject to the dictation of a state ministry.

An election can be regarded as a serious test of the will of the people only if full freedom of speech, press, and agitation is assured to all parties and groups and, more especially, if voters who desire to do so are permitted to organize in parties. The workers cannot be said to enjoy freedom of trade-union organization in Russia, where the trade-unions are dominated by the ruling Communist Party, or in Germany and Italy, where the labor organizations are supervised by the state. Genuine freedom of trade-union organization is only found in countries where the members of the unions, without any prompting from the state or the ruling party, freely select their officials and representatives on a democratic basis. Freedom of religion implies, besides the right to hold church services, the right of believers in any creed or, for that matter, in any philosophical idea, including atheism, to advocate their views in speech and press and to establish and maintain, with voluntary contributions, educational and welfare institutions.

Given this definition, I think it is or should be a matter of common knowledge that liberty, with some inevitable qualifications and defects, does prevail, in the main, in the United States and Great Britain, with its self-governing Dominions, in France and Scandinavia, Belgium and Holland, Switzerland and Czechoslovakia. The rest of Europe is now delivered over to communist, fascist and semi-fascist methods of rule. It is an equally obvious, if regrettable, fact that, as regards political and individual liberty, the clock has very definitely been set back, by comparison with pre-war standards, in several leading European countries. The scales in pre-war Germany were weighted in favor of the aristocratic and propertied classes; but Germany under the Kaiser was a paradise for John Stuart Mill, compared with the Nazi Third Reich. The police in Imperial Germany was strict, but one never heard of the outrageous beatings of helpless prisoners which have become commonplaces in Nazi detention cells and concentration camps. And no one would have been more horrified than the correct bureaucrat of pre-war Germany at the spectacle which Berlin experienced during the June 30th "purge," when bands of black-uniformed SS Guards scoured Berlin shooting down marked political opponents very much as Scarface Al Capone's henchmen picked off opponents of his hegemony when he was lord of the Chicago underworld.

Italy before the war was a land where the relatively new parliamentary system functioned clumsily, where criminal secret societies flourished in some parts, and where trains sometimes failed to arrive and depart on time. Its leaders were not, however, committed to dogmatic glorification of war; and an Italian could speak his mind on public affairs without having to anticipate an enforced trip to a penal island or a beating, accompanied by an enforced dose of castor oil.

The Soviet regime has not been content with taking over intact the entire Tsarist technique of repressing "dangerous thoughts" (censorship, espionage, arbitrary arrest, and administrative banishment); it has greatly improved on it. The assassination of the Tsar was the gravest conceivable crime under the Russian old regime. When Alexander II, the Tsar who abolished serfdom, was killed, after repeated unsuccessful attempts on his life, by a group of terrorists, five persons, all unquestionably implicated in the assassination, were put to death. There were no "reprisals," in the form of arbitrary killings of other revolutionaries.

When Sergei Kirov, one of Stalin's chief lieutenants, was assassinated in 1934 one hundred and seventeen persons were shot, of whom only thirteen, so far as one could judge from the laconic Soviet official communiqués on the killings after secret court-martial trials, were actually charged with complicity. The others were merely "counter-revolutionaries," for whose "liquidation" Kirov's death provided a convenient excuse. Quite recently sixteen more individuals, including two of Lenin's oldest disciples, Gregory Zinoviev and Leo Kamenev, were put to death, for alleged complicity in the assassination of Kirov and in alleged abortive plots against the lives of Stalin and some of his other associates. So, if the life of a Tsar called for five victims, that of a Soviet sub-dictator demanded at least one hundred and thirty-three.

These comparative figures on the punishment of political crime are by no means the only indication that the Soviet regime has gone far beyond its autocratic predecessor in terrorist repression. One cannot find in Tsarist legislation any parallel for the Soviet law of August 7, 1932, prescribing the death penalty for theft of state property (which in Russia means almost all property), or for the decree issued in the summer of 1934, under which innocent dependents of any Soviet citizen who flees from the country are to be punished with five years of banishment to Siberia.

It is scarcely necessary to prove that fascism controverts almost every detail of the definition of liberty which I have outlined. The speeches and writings of Hitler and Mussolini are filled with expressions of contempt for majority rule, for freedom of individual criticism, for any organization outside the framework of the all-embracing state; Mussolini in one burst of Latin exuberance envisages fascism as trampling on "the decaying corpse of liberty."

Fascist theory and practice have been quite consistent, at least in this respect. The accession to power of Mussolini in Italy and of Hitler in Germany has been followed by the substitution of farcical plebiscites for free elections. No critical discussion is permitted in connection with these plebiscites; all propaganda is for the existing regime. Any kind of opposition political activity, such as the holding of meetings or the circulation of leaflets, is strictly proscribed by the police and, if detected, is punished by imprisonment, not infrequently accompanied by beating and torture. It is not surprising, under these circumstances, that the results of the plebiscites reveal an outward unanimity of sentiment that is never attainable where people are free to express their real political preferences without coercion.

The "parliaments" which now exist in Germany and in Italy are as much of a parody of the true spirit of democratic institutions as the "elections" which bring them into being. A group of several hundred deputies, properly uniformed in black or brown shirts, as the case may be, snap to attention when the *Führer* or the *Duce* appears, punctuate his address with dutiful bellows of applause, laugh vociferously when the great man indulges in humor, pass unanimously every law that is submitted for their consideration, and quickly disperse to their homes. The whole ceremony suggests a military review rather than a popular deliberative assembly, and is vividly symbolic of the barracks stamp which fascism imposes on all thought and activity.

No one abroad is apt to be taken in by these "unanimous" plebiscites and drill-sergeant "parliaments"; and Mussolini and Hitler deserve credit for acknowledging the fully dictatorial character of their regimes, even if they do resort to a kind of fascist metaphysics in an effort to prove that their methods give their peoples the highest and most desirable kind of freedom.

The position in the Soviet Union calls for more consideration because of the recent promulgation of a new Constitution which promises, among other desirable things, "freedom of speech, freedom of the press, freedom of assembly and holding mass meetings, freedom of street processions and demonstrations, inviolability of persons and homes." The Constitution also does away with the former unequal system of voting, under which the city population possessed five times the voting power of the peasants, and prescribes "universal, equal and direct suffrage by secret ballot."

Were this Constitution to be genuinely implemented, the Soviet Union would deserve a place not among the dictatorships, but among the democracies of the world. Unfortunately, there are the strongest reasons for believing that all these glowing assurances of full democratic liberties will not be, and indeed cannot be, carried into effect. The Soviet Constitution is likely to rank with Litvinov's pledge to President Roosevelt to "prevent the activity on its territory of any organization which is working for the overthrow of the United States Government" (a pledge that obviously, if words mean anything, referred to the Communist International) as a document to be interpreted in a highly Pickwickian sense—in other words, not to be taken seriously.

The Ethiopian lurking in the woodpile of fine-sounding liberal phrases in which the Constitution abounds is the special status of the Communist Party. Anyone who possesses even the most elementary knowledge of the realities of Soviet politics knows that the Party and its various organs are much more important in influencing the course of public affairs than the various nominally elected Soviet legislative and administrative bodies, the functions of which are set down in such exhaustive detail in the Constitution.

The Political Bureau of the Party, which consists of Stalin and his nine chief associates, not the Council of People's Commissars, is the source of all important decisions of foreign and internal policy. The Press Department of the Central Committee of the Communist Party gives instructions on news and editorial policies to the Soviet newspapers, all of which, it may be noted, are publicly owned and all of which are edited by Communists. Going farther down the line of the Soviet administrative system, one finds that it is not the president of the local township or county Soviet, who is formally elected by popular vote, but the secretary of the Party committee who is the final authority in critical decisions.

The absolute monopoly of political power enjoyed by the Communist Party is further indicated by the fact that membership in this body is a prerequisite not only for the holding of political posts of any consequence, but also for high executive appointments in the huge administrative economic bureaucracy which manages Russia's industry, transportation, trade, and finance. No other party or political organization is tolerated; the political police has been very faithful in living up to the spirit of Lenin's remark that there might be any number of parties in Russia, provided that the Communist Party was in power and all the other parties in prison. The two earlier Soviet Constitutions contain no reference to the Communist Party. The present Constitution characterizes the position of the Party in the following rather general terms:

The most active and politically conscious citizens from among the working class and other strata of the toilers unite in the Communist Party of the Soviet Union, which is the vanguard of the toilers in their struggle to strengthen and develop the socialist system and which represents the leading core of all organizations of the workers, both social and state.

This conveys a very pale and imperfect idea of the Communist domination of every phase of activity in the Soviet Union which is the most important single fact about the character of the Soviet state. The membership of the Communist Party, at last reports, was in the neighborhood of two million. Now the domination of one hundred and seventy million people by a single party numbering about two million is quite incompatible with the theory and practice of democracy. The incompatibility becomes still more glaring if one considers that even within this ruling organization of two million real power is centralized in a very few men at the top, with Stalin at the apex. The rank-and-file Communist, the worker, say, in the Putilov factory, or the organizer of a collective farm in Ukraina has no voice in shaping higher Party policies. He is bound by the iron discipline which has always been a characteristic of the Party; and in recent years this discipline has become entirely indistinguishable from the personal will of Stalin.

Independent thinking is one of the gravest crimes in the Communist calendar. Party members who express dissent with the official "Party line" invite, at the least, expulsion from the Party, which often carries with it loss of employment; imprisonment, exile, even shooting are the penalties for the incorrigibly recalcitrant. There is not, therefore, any prospect of an evolution toward democracy through a relaxation of the dictatorial regime within the Party itself; the most recent comment in "Pravda," the official Party organ, and other Soviet newspapers, far from suggesting that freedom of speech within the Party might be a desirable prelude to the introduction of the new Constitution, clamors for a more ruthless witch-hunt of Trotzkyists and other heretics.

What would the guaranties of freedom of speech, press, assembly and personal liberty in the American Constitution be worth if all power in the American state were permanently vested in a single party, and if this party tolerated no criticism, debate, or open differences of opinion within its own ranks? Obviously very little; and the same characterization may reasonably be made of the shower of paper liberties which has suddenly descended on the surprised and probably sceptical heads of Soviet citizens. One feels that the framers of the instrument have slightly overdone their task; they have promised too much, and with too many flourishes.

Article 125, for instance, not content with assuring "freedom of speech, freedom of the press, freedom of assembly and of holding mass meetings, freedom of street processions and demonstrations," adds the following supplementary guaranty:

These rights of the citizens are ensured by placing at the disposal of the toilers and their organizations printing presses, supplies of paper, public buildings, the streets, means of communication and other material requisites for the exercise of these rights.

Hitler and Mussolini are quite willing to assure printing presses and supplies of paper for their party propaganda organs, to provide public buildings for National Socialist and Fascist rallies, and to rope off the streets periodically for Brown Shirt and Black Shirt parades. Freedom of speech, press, and assembly depends on whether these facilities are accorded to opposition groups.

A few hypothetical questions may help to test the validity of the promises contained in the Soviet Constitution. Will the Menshevik, or Moderate Socialist, leaders Dan and Abramovitch, who have consistently opposed terrorism and foreign intervention, but who disagree with certain Communist theories and practices be able to leave their émigré retreat in Paris and return to Moscow, with the assurance of having "a printing press and supplies of paper" with which to publish a journal setting forth their views? American Communists can hire a hall in any large city for the purpose of denouncing President Roosevelt and the capitalist system. What would be the chances of any dissatisfied group of Soviet citizens who tried to engage a hall for the purpose of criticizing Stalin and the socialist, or state-capitalist, system in the Soviet Union? How far would the right of "street processions and demonstrations" hold good if a body of Soviet workers, indignant at the speed-up methods of the Stakhanov movement, decided to hold a public protest? Or what would have been the fate of any idealistic Communists or opponents of imperialism who held a mass meeting in order to denounce the Soviet shipments of oil to aid Mussolini in overrunning Ethiopia? It will be surprising indeed if Soviet citizens, well disciplined by almost two decades of the Cheka and the now renamed Gay-Pay-Oo, decide to make any rash use of their new theoretical rights.

It may be contended that, while freedom of press, speech, and assembly must still be taken in a very qualified sense, the abolition of indirect and unequal suffrage, the introduction of the secret ballot, and the assurances of inviolability of persons and homes represent definite gains. Here again, however, it seems doubtful whether there will be much change in the *status quo*. The inequality in voting rights as between the urban and the rural population in practice has been much less important than it would have been in countries where elections are seriously contested. The sole probable change as a result of the abolition of the inequality is that more Communists working in rural areas will be elected to the Congress of Soviets. Inasmuch as these Congresses possess in practice no initiative rights and their functions are confined to listening to long reports by Commissars (Soviet Cabinet Ministers) and ratifying, always unanimously, any measures which may be laid before them, this possible change in their personnel is of minor importance. It is significant that Hitler and Mussolini have not found it necessary to resort either to open voting or to discriminatory franchise regulations in order to register their triumphant plebiscites. Give a single party complete control of the state machinery, outlaw all opposition parties and groups as "counterrevolutionary," and "elections," if they deserve the name, are certain to be tame and mechanical affairs.

As for the guaranties against arbitrary arrest, searches of homes, and opening of mail, it may be noted that civil and political liberties, such as freedom of speech, press, assembly, and elections and security against arbitrary arrests and searches, are, as a rule, indissoluble. They either exist *in toto* or they do not exist at all. Full freedom of speech, press, and voting is the sole adequate safeguard for the individual against the violence of the state. It is difficult to believe that practices which have become second nature to the Soviet political police will be or can be abandoned overnight, or that constitutional provisions about "the inviolability of the homes of citizens and secrecy of correspondence" will be allowed to interfere with such man hunts as the present one for suspected Trotzkyists.

In short, the new promises of the Soviet Constitution seem destined to rank, in validity, with an assurance that was incorporated in earlier versions of the instrument; namely, that each Soviet Republic "reserves the right freely to secede from the U.S.S.R." The "right to secede" is a barren mockery unless public advocacy of secession is permitted. There have been quite a number of nationalists who desired secession or at least a greater measure of autonomy in all the Soviet Republics, especially in Ukraina and Georgia. But any Ukrainian or Georgian who was caught by the Gay-Pay-Oo exercising his implied constitutional right to advocate secession was shot or imprisoned. There is little reason to suppose that the fate of any Soviet citizen who takes too seriously the new constitutional assurances of freedom of press, speech, and assembly will be different. The new Soviet Constitution must be interpreted primarily as part of the Soviet tactical maneuver to win sympathy in the democratic countries, since at the present time its most formidable potential enemy is fascist Germany. Unless there is an extraordinary and truly revolutionary change in Soviet administrative practice, of which there is no sign up to the present time, the maneuver is likely to impress only the very gullible.

What are the origins of the revolt against liberty that has swept over so large a part of the European continent? What lessons for the future can be drawn from a brief retrospective examination of the rise to power of Bolshevism in Russia, Fascism in Italy, and National Socialism in Germany? For it is in the governmental systems of these states that the really formidable challenge to democracy and individual liberty is embodied. The conservative rule which has long prevailed in Hungary, the shaky corporative state which has been patched up in Austria, the semi-fascist regime in Poland, the varying degrees of dictatorship which prevail in the Baltic and Balkan states are by comparison neither interesting nor important. Only in the Soviet Union, Germany, and Italy does one find the passion, zeal, and ruthlessness of new faiths, the working out of new conceptions of government and social philosophy.

All the leading post-war dictatorships are, in different ways, children of the World War. Had there been no such conflict it is most unlikely that the little known exiled revolutionary, Lenin, or the housepainter, Hitler, or the itinerant socialist agitator, Mussolini, would have found themselves in control of the destinies of their respective nations.

It was the war, rather than any human agency, that overthrew the Tsarist system, elaborately buttressed as it was by spies and police. It was the gigantic scope of the war that brought into sharp relief the incurable incompetence of the bureaucracy; sowed defection among officers and conservative statesmen who, in normal times, were the staunchest supporters of the Imperial regime; put guns into the hands of millions of revolutionary workers and peasants; reduced to relative impotence the normally strong police; in every way paved the way for the crumbling of the whole edifice of autocracy, for sheer lack of defenders, in March, 1917.

And Lenin, a realistic genius in gauging Russian political moods and possibilities, despite the obstinate doctrinaire mistakes which he often committed in estimating the chances of social revolution in other lands, realized immediately the opportunities which the crash of Tsarism and the emergence of a weak, inexperienced liberal regime opened up for his revolutionary ambition. By ruling out from the beginning any idea of compromise with the Provisional Government, by placing the Bolshevik Party, which he led, at the head of the mass demands for the end of the war, for the handing over of the land to the peasants, for workers' control of industry, by timing correctly the final stroke for power in November, he transformed Russia into the world's first socialist experimental laboratory.

The struggle was long and bitter; years of ferocious civil war and economic collapse led up to the huge famine of 1921–1922 and caused a temporary abandonment of some of the more extreme features of Soviet economic policy. But a resumption of the "socialist offensive" in 1929, again accompanied by intensified administrative ruthlessness, great privations, and actual famine in 1932–1933, completed the reorganization of the Russian economic order along socialist lines by bringing the great majority of the peasants into the so-called collective farm system, where the status of the peasant was that of a hired laborer, working under strict state control, not that of an independent small producer.

The basic economic transformation achieved by the Russian Bolshevik Revolution was from private initiative to universal state or public ownership and operation. While many features of capitalist technique have been preserved and some of them—such as inequality in compensation, piecework methods of payment, and bonuses—have been strengthened recently, private ownership and private profit, apart from compensation for services rendered, have been eliminated from Soviet industry, trade, transportation, mining, agriculture, and other fields of economic activity. Hand in hand with this thoroughgoing collectivization of economic life has gone the creation of an absolute political dictatorship, with the ruling Communist Party as an obedient instrument in the hands of Lenin's successor, Stalin, who concentrates in his hands an unparalleled combination of political and economic power.

Mussolini and Hitler, like Lenin, took advantage of the war, but in a somewhat different way. Italy, even more than most other European countries, experienced a great upsurge of social discontent during the years immediately after the war. Some developments in 1919 and 1920 suggested Russia in the year of revolutionary dissolution, 1917. The labor movement was dominated by socialism of an extreme type. Strikes, riots, acts of individual violence were constantly occurring. Perhaps the climax of this post-war radicalism was reached in 1920, when the workers occupied a considerable number of factories in northern Italy and the Government was unable to force them to evacuate. Ultimately this venture in syndicalism broke down because of natural difficulties with finance, technical direction, and supplies of raw material. But that it could be successfully carried out was indicative of the turbulent spirit of the time.

In revolutionary enterprise, as in other human affairs, there is a tide that must be taken if reaction and disaster are to be avoided. Lenin caught this tide in Russia; he carried out his coup at the moment when the upswing of revolutionary enthusiasm in the masses of workers and soldiers was at its height and the paralysis of morale in the Kerensky Government was complete. It is difficult to say at what moment, if at any time, Italy's radical Socialists would have stood the best chance of overthrowing the Government. But their tactics of irregular violence, if they did not lead to revolution, were calculated to provoke reaction.

The leader and beneficiary of this reaction was Benito Mussolini, a former revolutionary Socialist who had turned ardently nationalistic during the war. Starting from insignificant beginnings, Mussolini's fascist organization (the name was derived from the *fasces,* or bundles of rods, carried by the old Roman lictors) grew by leaps and bounds, winning more and more support among ex-officers and soldiers and the middle-class youth. Mussolini's programme was one of extreme nationalism, wide social reform, class collaboration instead of class struggle, and subordination both of labor and of capital to the interests of the Italian people as a whole, represented by a strong state.

Unlike the old-fashioned conservative generals and admirals who vainly tried to resist Bolshevism in Russia, Mussolini was a crowd orator, a man who could talk to the masses in their own language, who could paint his programme not as a mere restoration of the *status quo* but as a great revolutionary venture, the beginning of a new chapter in Italian history. He was helped by the split between the minority of Italian Socialists who accepted dictation from

Moscow and joined the Third International and the majority who, while avowing revolutionary objectives, declined to accept the stiff conditions laid down by the Third International for admission to membership. And when the tide was flowing in his direction, when, after years of savage street fights, ambushes, and clashes, his followers were sufficiently numerous and well organized to cow the Socialists and Communists into passivity by beatings and doses of castor oil, he did not miss his opportunity. His March on Rome, in 1922, terminating in his formal appointment as Premier by the King, opened a new era for Italy, as Lenin's seizure of power five years before had been one of the most important landmarks in Russian history. Fascism has dominated Italy for fourteen years. A new generation has grown up under its influence. Mussolini has not abolished private ownership in industry and agriculture; but he has assured the state a decisive voice in controlling the main lines of national economic development. Capital and labor in the main branches of economic activity are organized in syndicates, with the Fascist Party wielding a decisive influence in these organizations. Between the formal control exercised by various state departments and the pressure which is exercised by local Fascist organizations, little old-fashioned freedom of initiative remains to the Italian business man. The rugged individualist who wants to run his own business in his own way is probably only a little less unhappy in Italy than in the Soviet Union.

The third major post-war revolution occurred in Germany in 1933. It followed the Italian, not the Soviet, model, although with some distinctive features such as the intense stimulation of anti-Semitic feeling, which may be attributed to differences between Italian and German conditions and psychology. Although he lacked Mussolini's past as a revolutionary agitator, Adolf Hitler emerged from the World War in which he had served as a volunteer in the German Army with a *Weltanschauung* very similar to that of the Italian dictator. Like Mussolini, he despised democracy and pacifism, exalted the nation above everything, abhorred Marxism and class warfare, while believing that a new type of social organization could give the manual workers an honored place along with other classes within the framework of the united nation.

Hitler's first bid for power, the *Putsch* which he launched in a Munich beer hall in November, 1923, was a tragi-comic fiasco. The Premier of Bavaria, von Kahr, and the local commander of the *Reichswehr*, or regular army, von Lossow, whom Hitler had coerced into declaring solidarity with him at the moment when he proclaimed his uprising, repudiated him as soon as they were free from pressure. The *Reichswehr* fired on and dispersed his followers; and Hitler himself was sentenced to a term of im-

prisonment in a fortress, where he wrote the auto-
biography that has now become the most widely
read book in Germany, "Mein Kampf."

The first period of Germany's post-war chaos and
despair, which reached its climax with the French
occupation of the Ruhr and came to an end with the
adoption of the Dawes Plan and the subsequent
improvement in the political and economic situation,
did not bring Hitler into power. His chance came
later, when the world crisis affected Germany with
special severity, partly because of the overexpan-
sion of some industries during the period of false
prosperity generated by a reckless inflow of foreign
capital, partly because Germany's reserve savings
had been bled white by war, reparations payments,
and inflation.

As wages and salaries were cut, as the income of
the peasants sharply declined, while unemployment
grew to staggering proportions, the stage was set
for the triumph of anyone who advocated desperate
measures to meet a desperate situation. It seemed
to be a race between Hitler and the German Communists; but the latter were soon left far behind.
They were handicapped by their close identification
with Moscow, by the narrow class basis of their appeal, by the widespread if erroneous belief that Social Democrats had been largely responsible for the
defeat in 1918.

Hitler, on the other hand, an unrivalled mass

orator, struck a responsive chord in almost every class with his sweeping promises and vague practical programme. The aureole of the forgotten soldier of the World War was about him; his mystical faith in Germany's greatness and in the need for absolute German unity was widely popular; his indefinite anticapitalism and very positive anti-Semitism fitted in very well with the mood of great numbers of ruined and embittered middle-class Germans.

The result was that Hitler was able to give a striking exhibition of how democracy could be destroyed by democratic means. Warned by the experience of 1923, Hitler held back his more impetuous followers who would have risked a second coup. Throughout the years of ever worsening crisis, 1929, 1930, 1931, 1932, he watched the votes piling up ever higher for the National Socialist candidates at the ballot-box.

And finally, when Hindenburg's effort to restore old-fashioned conservative government, with *Junker* aristocrats in key positions, failed—partly because such a government could gain no broad basis of popular support, partly because individual intrigues and jealousies interfered—Hitler came into power quite legally as Premier by appointment of President Hindenburg and consolidated his position by winning, with his Nationalist allies, a scant majority in Germany's last free election, in March, 1933. The German people has had no chance since that time to reverse its judgment, if it so desired. The whole apparatus of modern-style dictatorship, annihilation of the opposition press, killing, beating and imprisonment of opposition leaders, destruction of all parties except the ruling one, was quickly clamped down on the country.

In National Socialist Germany, as in Fascist Italy, private capitalism, in the sense of individual ownership of factories, farms, banks, mines, stores, etc., has not been destroyed. But it has been closely curbed and controlled. The alleged regimentation of private enterprise during the Roosevelt Administration, which has been so much denounced in American business circles, has been very mild compared with the measures which have been applied in Germany. The following summary of the position of the German business man by a foreign observer[1] gives an indication of how incompatible fascism is with the idea that business should be free from outside interference and regulation:

Most business men find it advisable to keep on the right side of the local party authorities. By no stretch of the imagination can their property be called their own. The State suggests or limits extensions of plant or new construction; it fixes most prices as well as wages, endeavouring to prevent price increases; it compels companies increasing dividends to invest an equal amount in Government securities; it organises compulsory cartels; it dictates the use

[1] "The German Revolution," by H. Powys Greenwood, p. 222 (London: George Routledge & Sons, 1934).

of domestic instead of foreign raw materials. The party presses for new men to be taken on, for longer holidays with pay, for free Labour Front uniforms for the workers, for higher bonuses, and the like. No directors of important, or even of unimportant, private concerns are appointed without the tacit assent of the State and the Nazi Party.

Labor is similarly coerced. There are no independent trade-unions; and the representation of the workers' interests is left in the hands of National Socialist factory organizations or of "councils of confidence," in which National Socialists play a leading rôle. The Nazi local organizations are, of course, subject to party discipline and cannot agitate for wage increases, even to meet an increasing cost of living, if the order is handed down from above that, in the interests of the nation, such increases must be forgone.

So there are a number of common origins in the political and economic systems which embody the post-war revolt against liberty. All three revolutions—the Russian, the Italian, and the German—are most closely linked up with the war, that unrivalled school of violence and direct action. All occurred in times of great stress and suffering, when the Russian, Italian, and German peoples might fairly be regarded as shell-shocked and as ready to grasp at any straw which promised relief. All were based on a more or less conscious abandonment of individualism, on the conception that the state, in one form or another, should wield greater power over the individual and at the same time insure the individual security.

Revolution is usually thought of as a reaction against tyranny; and some revolutions in history conform quite well to this definition. It is highly significant that not one of these three modern revolutions, all of which have contracted, not enlarged, the sphere of human liberty, can be interpreted on this basis. The bitterest critic of the governmental systems which preceded the coming of Bolshevism, Fascism, and National Socialism, cannot accuse Kerensky in Russia, or Facta (the Italian Premier at the time of Mussolini's coup), or the heads of the various Cabinets which governed Germany under the very liberal Weimar Constitution of employing undue measures of severity in dealing with political opponents. Indeed, if the methods which Lenin and Stalin, Hitler and Mussolini employed in "liquidating" political opposition after they came into power had been applied to them when they were themselves agitators, they would all have been shot at least half a dozen times. So the modern-style revolution seems to develop not when a government is oppressively strong, but when it is so hopelessly weak that it is an easy prey for an organized revolutionary minority with a whole-hearted desire to seize power, a complete absence of democratic scruples and an adequate supply of machine guns and other lethal weapons.

If success, in the sense of putting a group of people in power and keeping them there, is the standard by which revolutions are to be judged, then the new regimes in the Soviet Union, Germany, and Italy must be regarded as having passed the test. A good many human eggs have been smashed in the process —most of all, certainly, in Russia, with Germany second and Italy third in the matter of casualties of the overturns. But the Bolshevik, National Socialist, and Fascist omelettes have been cooked to a turn. The most uncompromising opponents of these new-style dictatorships, in so far as they retain any trace of realistic judgment, do not anticipate their downfall, except possibly as one of the by-products of the hypothetical next world war. They are safe against any domestic outbreak of discontent. Fascist Italy has successfully passed the test of mobilization and war—not a very glorious war, to be sure, but one that was complicated to some extent by the half-hearted sanctions imposed by the League of Nations. The Soviet regime has emerged unshaken from the much harder ordeal of its own far-reaching internal experiments: it was able to destroy economically and to some extent physically whole classes of its population (such as the kulaks, or former well-to-do peasants, and the private traders) and to allow a huge famine, with millions of victims, to take its course in 1932 and 1933 without arousing any serious internal revolt. All three dictatorial systems have made noteworthy strides in armament and in training and preparing their peoples for war; their relative weight in the concert of European powers has correspondingly increased.

What are the secrets of the strength and stability of the communist and fascist governments? What differentiates them sharply from democracies, on the one hand, and from old-fashioned, conservative, authoritarian types of government, on the other? What, in short, is the new technique of tyranny?

Chapter II

THE NEW TECHNIQUE OF TYRANNY

THE contrast between freedom and tyranny is at least as old as the wars between the Greeks and the Persians. But the forms of this contrast vary. Before the war the typical enemy of liberty was the traditional autocrat or the ambitious soldier who succeeded in making himself a small-scale Napoleon with the support of his troops. Both the absolute monarch and the upstart military dictator ruled with the aid of their troops and their police and were mainly concerned to detect and stamp out any signs of political activity among their subjects. A logical corollary of this system of government was the indifference, not to say antipathy, with which a Russian Tsar or a Mexican dictator of the type of Díaz was apt to regard any attempt to spread education among the masses of the people. Fearing above all things "dangerous thoughts," to borrow the delightful phrase coined in all seriousness by a Japanese bureaucrat, the old-style absolute ruler distinctly preferred that the people under his sway should do as little thinking of any kind as possible. This attitude is admirably epitomized in the exclamation of an early American colonial governor:

"Thank God there is not a printing-press in Virginia."

There are still types of government which, to a greater or lesser degree, rely on traditionalism and mere police repression to keep the lower orders in subjection. But these methods clearly belong to the horse-and-buggy age of tyranny.

The communist-fascist technique of remaining in power is far more up-to-date, subtle, and formidable. It is based first of all on a recognition of the tremendous possibilities of state-monopolized propaganda in an age when most people go to school, read newspapers, listen to radio broadcasts, and attend the movies. Censors and book burners can do a good deal; but they cannot altogether reverse or abolish the effects of scientific progress and discovery. What the post-war dictatorship does is to harness the most modern devices of publicity to its propaganda chariot. Printing-presses are not smashed; they are all utilized to spread far and wide the same brand of political, economic, and social doctrine.

People are not forbidden to possess radio sets or to go to the movies. But nothing goes on the air in the Soviet Union, Germany, or Italy that could possibly offend, respectively, Stalin, Hitler, and Mussolini. The Russian can go to a film and see Communists heroically toiling for the country's upbuilding and finally prevailing over the dark intrigues of fascist villains. The German may be simultaneously witnessing a film of precisely the same ideological content, with the rôles of hero and villain reversed. The schools and the press are also exploited to the limit as means of teaching people, from the cradle to the grave, to think and behave in the way which the ruling system demands.

If a new Machiavelli should arise to expound in lucid outline the new technique of tyranny, his wisdom would not be confined to the milder methods of mass hypnosis and persuasion. Communism and fascism must bulldoze as well as bamboozle, coerce as well as cajole. In this connection the new Machiavelli would doubtless suggest what Stalin, Hitler, Mussolini, and their aides already know: that few individuals possess within them the stuff of heroes and martyrs.

Consequently a regime of calculated frightfulness, which does not give its victims even the consolation of public martyrdom, a system of secret killings without public trial, of wholesale brutality in concentration camps, of universal espionage, is certain to break all but the strongest spirits, to make impossible organized opposition to the sacrifices which the omnipotent rulers demand of the masses—for their own good, of course. Experience in all the three countries that have adopted the new technique of government by unlimited propaganda plus unlimited terror indicates that a part of the population becomes converted to a belief in the existing order, that another and probably larger part learns the wisdom of keeping its collective mouth shut, that obstinate dissidents who are not killed outright are cowed and crushed, and that the credulous foreign visitor who comes to see and to admire has unrivalled chances for making a fool of himself.

It is this combination of mass propaganda and its accompaniment, mass organization, with terrorism that accounts for the simultaneous truth of two propositions about the communist and fascist regimes which, at first sight, appear contradictory. Their records of brutal and ruthless repression, as I pointed out in the preceding chapter, are much worse than those of their predecessors, no matter what standard of comparison is taken: the number of political executions, or of persons in prisons and concentration camps for alleged opposition to the government, or of émigrés who have been obliged to flee from the country. Yet it is equally true that each of the three systems has behind it a large body of enthusiastic supporters, such as governments which practice humaner methods often lack. There can be no doubt, for instance, that the present Austrian Government, although it has been far more decent in its methods of treating political opponents, is much weaker, as regards popular support, than the Hitler regime in Germany. Ability to inspire a large body of followers with faith in a cause for which no sacrifice seems too great and no atrocity too revolting is, of course, a primary consideration in this connection. The leaders of Russian Communism, Italian Fascism, and German National Socialism have possessed this gift, and have fortified it by developing a routine system of whipping up enthusiasm among their supporters and striking terror into their opponents.

Nothing makes either a communist or a fascist so angry as to be likened to the other. The obvious antagonisms between the two systems at first sight may overshadow the likenesses. Fascists are shot or imprisoned at sight in the Soviet Union; Communists in Germany and Italy. Fascist sympathy has been openly expressed for the conservative rebels, Communist sympathy for the radical Government in Spain. The leaders of the Soviet Union and of Germany exchange denunciations of each other's systems.

Yet hostility is no proof of unlikeness. Foch and Hindenburg were bitter-end opponents in the World War. But both cherished much the same code of soldierly virtue; both admired courage and patriotism, abhorred pacifism, placed their country's military interests above every other consideration. There is more psychological sense than might appear at first sight in the National Socialist idea that the "front soldiers" of the warring countries, who were formerly fighting each other in the trenches, develop much the same outlook on life and now can readily be friends.

The striking similarities of administrative method between the communist and fascist states certainly make these two systems far more akin to each other than either is to a democratic country. It may or may not be true that Soviet officials in Berlin, after the advent of Hitler, began to whisper among themselves: "Now we feel more at home here." But that Germany after the coming of Hitler became vastly more similar to the Soviet Union than it had been under the Weimar Republic is beyond any reasonable doubt or dispute.

Before 1933 it was a tremendous relief, physical and psychological, to go from hungry, spy-ridden Moscow, where people were constantly "disappearing," to be reported later as "liquidated" or consigned to concentration camps, where letters were opened and telephones tapped and squalor and overcrowding were the general rule, to clean, orderly Berlin, where the shops were stocked with goods, where there was no fear of involving a German friend of any political persuasion in difficulties with the police by calling on him, where any kind of idea, from Bolshevism to extreme nationalism, could be freely discussed. The physical contrast between the two capitals has remained since the coming of National Socialism. It reflects differences of national temperament and character. The German is naturally neat, efficient, punctual; the Russian is slovenly, indifferent to comfort, apt to combine grandiose dreams for the future with very defective accomplishment in the present.

But the psychological contrast between the two cities has largely disappeared. Now Berlin, like Moscow, is ruled by a curious combination of mass enthusiasm and individual fear. Huge parades and demonstrations seem to attest the strength and popularity of the existing regimes. But in Germany as in Russia, the individual, unless he is completely identified with the ruling group, prefers not to discuss politics, looks around with apprehension if he is talking in a public place, not infrequently is definitely indisposed to meet a foreigner.

The list of parallels in political practice between German National Socialism and Italian Fascism on one hand, and Russian Communism on the other, is long and significant. First of all, is the system of government by means of a single party—any attempt to organize an opposition party or a dissident group within the ruling party being treated as "counter-revolution" and repressed with the utmost severity. In recruiting the membership of their parties Stalin, Hitler, and Mussolini emphasize quality above numbers; there is no desire to make membership in the parties universal. On the contrary, the Russian Communist, the Italian Fascist, the German National Socialist is regarded, in theory, as a mem-

ber of a small élite minority of the nation, entitled
to rule because of his greater devotion to the cause
and his willingness to make sacrifices for it. Hitler
stated on one occasion that, while he hoped the day
would come when "every decent German" would be
a National Socialist in sympathy, only a minority
should belong to the Party. The Soviet Constitution defines the membership of the Communist Party
as consisting of "the most active and politically conscious citizens."

The idea of a state ruled by a moral and intellectual élite has found its champions from Plato to
H. G. Wells. As a relief from the imperfections,
compromises, and disillusionments that followed the
general adoption of democratic institutions during
the nineteenth century its appeal is obvious. Serious
difficulties, however, crop up when the question arises
how the select minority is to be chosen.

The process of organization of the three ruling
parties of the present time has been remarkably similar, when one takes account of differences of Russian,
German, and Italian political development. Each
has its "old guard," with the typical characteristics
of pioneer fanatics of any new faith: absolute devotion to their cause and willingness to kill or be killed
for it, boundless energy, complete intolerance for
critics and dissenters. The Soviet Communist old
guard consists partly of the "underground" revolutionaries of Tsarist times, of the men and women

who faced the repeated arrests and sentences of exile and imprisonment in order to distribute illegal agitation literature and carry on surreptitious propaganda work, partly of outstanding figures in the Russian civil war. The Fascist and National Socialist old guards are largely recruited from former front-line officers and soldiers who acquired in the trenches of the World War the hardening in courage and in ruthlessness that came to Communists in the prison-cells of Tsarism and on the battlefields and execution cellars of Russia's savage civil war.

As all three ruling parties grew in size very greatly immediately before and after their accession to power the "old guard" members were outnumbered by newer recruits. However, most of the trusted counsellors of the three dictators, and most of the men in the highest administrative posts, belong to the older generations of the parties.

The ideal that every Communist, every National Socialist, and every Fascist should be a selfless enthusiast, concerned only for the triumph of his cause, was not and could not be realized, except in the case of a few exceptional individuals. One problem that none of the parties has been able to solve satisfactorily is that of the careerist, the man who would never have thought of attaching himself to a small group of persecuted revolutionaries, but who is quick to attach himself to the winning side after the new regime has been installed in power.

The evolution from the genuine idealism and enthusiasm which marked the first phase of all three revolutions to routine bureaucratism has been further hastened by the fact that in practice implicit obedience to the party leader has been a surer guaranty of advancement in the party than devotion to the original ideals of the movement. All three parties have had their heretics, who were not infrequently among the more thoughtful and idealistic party members. And in all three parties heretics who questioned the supreme authority of the party leader have been quickly and firmly suppressed.

The conservative French historian and philosopher, Taine, saw in the sending of Robespierre, Danton, Saint-Just, Hébert, and many other leaders of the French Revolution to the guillotine to which they had condemned so many others "the crocodile devouring its young." The Russian and German Revolutions have also devoured not only their opponents but many of their early leaders who subsequently fell out of step. Hitler's famous "blood purge" of June 30, 1934, which took the lives of such prominent National Socialists as Roehm, organizer of the Storm Troopers, Gregor Strasser, formerly a leading party theoretician and Edmund Heines, one of the most daring and ruthless of the commanders of the Storm Troopers, recently found its echo in Russia. Gregory Zinoviev and Leo Kamenev, two of Lenin's earliest associates, who for a time were bosses of the Communist organizations in Russia's two largest cities, Leningrad and Moscow, were shot down by a firing squad, while Mikhail Tomsky, formerly a member of the all-powerful Political Bureau of the Communist Party and head of the Soviet trade-unions, was harried into committing suicide. These were only the outstanding victims, in Germany and in Russia, of sweeping repressive measures which involved many more executions and still more sentences of imprisonment and banishment.

A common characteristic of the three post-war dictatorships is the emergence of an infallible and omnipotent *Vozhd, Duce* or *Führer* (to give the Russian, Italian and German terms for "leader"), who exercises over the ruling party the same sway that the party, in turn, wields over the country. In every case the absolutism of the leader has become stronger with the passing of time. Lenin was repeatedly publicly opposed at Party Congresses and some adverse votes were cast against Stalin at a Party Congress as late as 1925. Since that time unanimity has been the rule for Party Congresses as well as for Soviet Congresses. Mussolini was unable to control the Fascist Party in carrying out a truce in street fighting which he had arranged with Premier Bonomi before the march on Rome. But in recent years not a dissenting voice has made itself audible within the Fascist ranks. Criticism of Hitler within the Nazi ranks has been impressively stilled ever since the emphatic lesson of June 30. The same process, manifesting itself under three different systems, would seem to indicate the working of a general law of political development. And this law is that a revolutionary leader, who may be troubled by splits in his own ranks while he is still struggling for power, tends to become increasingly absolute and irresponsible after he has at his disposal all the resources of the modern state. Any opposition to him, even though it may be headed by influential veteran party members, is foredoomed to failure. He may be assassinated or he may be swept away by a cataclysm, such as a disastrous war, which would smash his whole system. He may not be successfully checked or controlled.

The character of the personal rule established by Stalin, Hitler, and Mussolini is distinctive, equally far removed from traditional autocracy and from democracy. On the one hand the authority of the leader, the abject servility of the tributes which are paid to him may fairly be said to exceed anything that was experienced at the most despotic European courts before the war. One suspects that Tsar Nicholas II would have been slightly embarrassed if any Russian author had addressed him in the terms of Byzantine adulation which the proletarian writer Avdyenko used to glorify Stalin at a recent Communist Party Congress:

Centuries shall elapse and the communist generations of the future will deem us the happiest of all mortals that have inhabited this planet throughout the ages, because we have seen Stalin the leader-genius, Stalin the Sage, the smiling, the kindly, the supremely simple. When I met Stalin, even at a distance, I throbbed with his forcefulness, his magnetism, and his greatness. I wanted to sing, to shriek, to howl from happiness and exaltation.

Alongside this lush outburst one may set the line which Italian school children must learn by heart and repeat over and over, "Mussolini is always right," and the remarkable declaration by a German Evangelical Bishop in 1934 that "June 30th had made clear, even to the blind, what I have always recognized: the unique greatness of *der Führer*."

Yet at the same time there is an element of social democracy about the personality of the modern-style dictator and the nature of his regime. Stalin's father was a Caucasian shoemaker, Hitler's a minor customs official, Mussolini's a blacksmith. Birth and wealth played no part in their rise to supreme power. And no one of these dictators has been credibly accused of abusing his power for the purpose of building up a large personal or family fortune. They have been cruel but not corrupt, merciless but not vulgar. And there is nothing hereditary or dynastic about their regimes. Hitler has no children; Mussolini's and Stalin's sons have never been mentioned as candidates for their fathers' seats of power. Any rank-and-file Communist, Fascist or National Socialist could theoretically succeed the present dictator although in actual practice the choice will be limited to a fairly narrow circle of eminent party functionaries and state officials.

The infallible leader and the single ruling party are by no means the sole common features of the three major post-war dictatorships. All of them enjoy much more support from the young than from the middle-aged. The Russian Revolution, the most violent and sweeping of the three, disrupted innumerable families, the sons and daughters joining the Union of Communist Youth and throwing themselves whole-heartedly into the task of "building socialism," while their fathers and mothers stand aloof, depressed by the hardships and horrified by the cruelties of the new order. In Germany and Italy also there is unmistakably a new spirit in the youth that has grown up under the spell of Hitler and Mussolini. In Russia, where the Soviet Government in 1937 will celebrate two decades of its existence, and in Italy, where Mussolini has dominated the country for fifteen years, it is almost inevitable that the youth should, in the main, be on the side of the new order. A whole generation has grown up knowing nothing else and subjected to a most intensive course of propaganda. From the kindergarten through the school and the university, the

Russian or Italian youth is taught to sing Communist or Fascist songs, to regard Stalin or Mussolini as the greatest man who ever lived, to consider the political and social system of his country as superior to any other. Germany's Third Reich has existed for a shorter period. But Hitler's movement, before it swept into power, had enlisted the ardent enthusiasm of a large part of the German youth. The majority of the university students were actively engaged in it. The Storm Troopers were a cross-section of Young Germany in which every class was strongly represented.

Exaltation of manual labor is another point in which there is little difference between the three dictatorships. In such prosaic things as food, clothing, and housing it cannot be said that any of them have done particularly well for labor or, indeed, for any other class in the population. But Stalin, Hitler, and Mussolini vie with one another in their tributes to the ennobling character of physical labor. The entire Soviet regime was originally based on the idea of the dictatorship of the proletariat, or manual working class, although real power always rested in the hands of the higher Communist bureaucracy and recently there has been a distinct tendency to abolish special privileges for manual workers. Hitler sees in compulsory labor service a means of breaking down German class distinctions; in the course of a speech at a May First celebration he declared:

We want to teach this German people by means of compulsory labor service that manual labor neither disgraces nor dishonors, but, like every other human activity, honors him who does it truly and honestly. And it is therefore our unalterable decision that every individual German, whoever he may be, whether he be rich and of high estate or poor, whether the son of a professor or of a factory laborer, shall once in his life do manual labor, in order that he may know what it is, in order that he may better be able to command because he has already learned how to obey.

Mussolini does not yield to either of his fellow-dictators in his glorification of labor; on some occasions he has set an example to the Italian people by stripping himself to the waist in the hot summer sun and helping to gather in the harvest.

The modern-style dictatorship is definitely and implacably anti-intellectual. Whether it is Goebbels in Germany or Kaganovitch in the Soviet Union, or some lieutenant of Mussolini in Italy, a favorite theme of communist-fascist oratory is the contrast between the splendid discipline of the workers and peasants in supporting the existing regime and the contemptible surreptitious grumbling of the intellectuals. It is an ironical commentary on the naïve enthusiasm of a certain type of left-wing intellectual in Western Europe and America for Russian communism in theory and practice that the Soviet Union has shot, jailed, and driven into exile a higher proportion of its educated class than any other country in the world. Germany under Hitler occupies second place in this respect, and Fascist Italy is probably third.

Dictatorships are as reticent with atrocity figures as they are profuse with statistics about real or imaginary achievements. But proof of the foregoing statement is easy to find. The number of Russian émigrés scattered over the world is in the neighborhood of a million, the number of German refugees about one hundred thousand, the number of Italian political exiles much smaller, probably not more than a few thousand. The proportion of educated men and women among the Russian émigrés is at least as high as it is among the Germans and Italians. So much for the comparative figures as regards exiles; and it may be noted that a man does not flee from his native country and take up the hard, poverty-stricken life of an exile in a foreign land except under overwhelming pressure.

So far as killings are concerned, neither Germany nor Italy, despite the many acts of violence and outrage which are associated with their regimes, has experienced anything like the wholesale shooting, without trial, of forty-eight Russian professors and experts in the food industry in 1930, of thirty-five employees of the Commissariat for Agriculture— many of them well known experts in agricultural theory—in 1933, or the many smaller batches of executions for alleged sabotage in industry, transport, and other branches of Soviet life. It was officially

announced a few years ago in the Soviet Union that
two thousand engineers had been arrested in connection with the alleged sabotage plot of the so-called
"Industrial Party." Here again the fascist states have
failed to keep up with their fellow dictatorship in
Russia.

⁓To be sure the new technique of tyranny requires
an intelligentsia of sorts; the big propaganda mills
cannot run without some lubricating oil of education. So the author, the teacher, the journalist who
toe the line and write and talk precisely as they are
told by the ruling party are materially fairly well
provided for in the Soviet Union, Germany, and
Italy. But Stalin, Hitler, and Mussolini are psycho-
logically quite correct when they see in the intellectual who thinks for himself and even, on occasion,
feels a moral obligation to express some critical idea,
the deadliest menace to their systems. What these
systems, which rely for their existence on mass emotional stimulation plus terrorism, naturally fear
above everything else is cool rational criticism, sober
deflation of their self-magnified achievements. Hence
there must be war to the death on the independent
intelligentsia.

The likenesses between the Soviet Union and Germany become much more numerous if one substi-
tutes race bias for class bias. The fate of the Jews
in Germany has been strikingly similar to that of the

kulaks, or former well-to-do peasants, and other proscribed classes in Russia. Indeed the new Machiavelli who some day may expound the up-to-date
technique of tyranny will probably lay down as one
of the rules of the modern dictator: "Always have at
hand a distinctive minority, too weak to offer resistance, prosperous enough to excite envy, for your devoted followers to torment and persecute. Such a
minority is especially useful when the people are
passing through hard times and need some diversion
for their minds."

The Jews have played this rôle in Germany, and
the kulaks in the Soviet Union; and Hitler and
Stalin have made the most of their opportunities in
this connection. It must be reckoned to Mussolini's
relative credit that he has not sought a scapegoat in
any special class or race in Italy. Like his fellow-
dictators, he has smashed his political opponents
ruthlessly. But he has not set out to compass the
"liquidation" of a whole class, like the Russian
kulaks, or of an entire racial minority, like the German Jews. It may be, of course, that the Abyssinians
have been doomed to fill the dictator's inescapable
need of a weak enemy to be crushed.

Many features of the treatment meted out to Jews
and kulaks have been completely identical: exclusion
from all public services, vilification in the press, discrimination in the matter of receiving social benefits,

denial to their children of admission to higher educational institutions. As in practically all cases where comparison is possible, the balance of ruthlessness is in favor of the Soviet Union. Jews are still able to carry on business, although under many handicaps, in Germany; the last Russian kulak has long been consigned to a concentration camp at forced labor or, if he was very lucky, has escaped to some part of the country where his identity is unknown, his house, land, and property being confiscated. The treatment of the German Jews has been merciless enough; yet any Russian kulak would have welcomed the opportunity enjoyed by the German Jew to leave the country with even a small part of his property.

While Germany's scapegoats have fared more mildly than Russia's, many features of the sordid and pitiful processes of race and class persecution are strangely similar. It would be difficult to imagine anything meaner than the state of mind suggested by the following word picture, cited from an article in the Nazi monthly, "Der Weltkampf," advocating the complete exclusion of Jewish children from the primary schools, because their presence is an obstacle to the success of anti-Semitic propaganda among the other pupils:

The young teacher, consumed with zeal, unsheathes his sword and calls a spade a spade. He quotes the Talmud, he refers to the stories about the Bible Patriarchs, seizes every opportunity for emphasizing the criminal rôle played by Jews in politics, he posts up pictures from the *Stürmer* [the most violent German anti-Semitic publication] and combats the legend of the so-called "decent Jew." He misses no chance of instilling into the hearts of his children hatred and contempt for the foreign parasite.

All this he does, and yet, unless he is gifted with exceptional powers of carrying conviction, the result may too easily be exactly the opposite of what he intended. For at the farthest and hindmost desk sits a little Jewish urchin, the helpless target of all the attacks on world Jewry. He can make no defense, but sits there clenching his fists and biting back his tears. Such a spectacle revolts the ever chivalrous German spirit, and it may well be not the worst of his class comrades who, for this reason, feel moved to champion the cause of the persecuted.

As an exhibit in race fanaticism this is pretty bad. Yet I can recall a very similar demonstration of class fanaticism which I witnessed in Russia. It was in the large Kolomna machine-building works in the winter of 1929–1930, when the drive to "liquidate the kulaks" was at its height. A fanatical woman, a Communist Party organizer, was addressing a group of young workers, who were supposed to go out into the country districts and help the local authorities in despoiling the wretched kulaks of their property and driving them from their homes. She specially stressed the point that there must be no mercy for their children, that they would grow up into kulaks some day, that they must also be driven from their homes and under no conditions allowed to enter any Soviet youth organizations or get employment in any state establishment. The whole spirit of her speech was precisely that of the Nazi article which I have cited.

The abundant nonsense that has been written in Russia since the Revolution about the "class line"— in literature, drama, statistics, philosophy and what not—finds a suitable echo in the "race line" that has been drawn in Germany. And the insistence on red-blooded proletarian origin as a favorable prerequisite of preferment in Russia is surely akin to the demand for a pure "Aryan" ancestral tree in Germany.

Some time ago a student, whose name will scarcely be remembered in scientific history, announced that, in his opinion, there were two distinct kinds of physics: Jewish physics and German physics. Needless to say, he stood whole-heartedly for German physics. One would have to go to Russia to find a match for this absurdity in the frequent declarations about "art on the class front" and the necessity for combating "bourgeois" tendencies in everything from architecture to statistics.

In view of the overwhelming force represented by the combination of unlimited repression with unlimited propaganda employed by the new-style totalitarian state, it is surprising that underground resistance still goes on. Yet there are still enough gallant zealots of their ideas and innocent people falsely denounced by the police to keep the prison-camps of the three lands crowded to overflowing. A more typical and safer form of protest, however, is the resort to contraband humor. Moscow, Berlin, and Rome all have their satirical jokes, which pass about without ever being written down; a complete collection of them would be not only a very funny book, but an excellent footnote to official history. Here one may give one specimen of the contraband joke from each country.

Let us begin with Russia. A music professor, looking tired and discouraged, meets an official of the Gay-Pay-Oo, or Political Police, who asks what is worrying him. The professor complains that his students are so unprepared that not one of them could tell him the name of the composer of Tschaikovsky's famous opera, "Eugene Onegin." "That certainly looks like counter-revolution and sabotage," says the Gay-Pay-Oo official. "We'll soon attend to that matter, professor." The two meet about a month later, and the official, beaming with pride, announces: "I told you the Gay-Pay-Oo would soon take care of this case. We arrested all the students in your class and, after we had held them in solitary confinement, varied by a few all-night examinations, we obtained signed confessions from several of them that they had written 'Eugene Onegin' themselves."

The German story refers to a letter, supposedly written by a Jewish resident of Germany to a relative abroad. The letter reads: "All is prosperous in the

Third Reich. No hair of a Jew's head has been touched. Uncle Moritz, who expressed a contrary opinion, was buried yesterday."

Italy's contribution to underground humor represents Mussolini as entering a moving-picture theatre incognito. His picture is thrown on the screen, and the audience rises and bursts into applause while he remains modestly seated. His neighbor leans over and touches him on the shoulder, saying: "I sympathize with you, and a good many of us feel just as you do. But—it would be safer to get up and join in the cheering."

It is in the field of governmental terrorism that the resemblance between the two main post-war types of dictatorship is most overwhelming and unmistakable. The homely old saying about the pot calling the kettle black applies equally to Communists, protesting against "Fascist barbarity" and to Fascists and National Socialists, extolling their regimes as the bulwarks of European civilization against Communism. It is quite true that there have been cases of Fascist barbarity; but the Communists, in view of their record in the sole country where they seized power, are the last people in the world who have any moral right to denounce it. It is equally true that a general spread of communism would be an irreparable blow to humanistic European culture and civilization. But Fascist systems that adopt almost every feature of the Communist technique of tyranny are not altogether plausible champions of this culture and civilization.

There is not a single trick of administrative repression and brutality that the fascist dictatorships have not learned, or could not have learned from the practice of the Soviet Union. And they have proved extremely apt pupils. Many books have been written about the mental and physical torments of individuals who have fallen into the clutches of the Soviet Gay-Pay-Oo (now renamed, but as active as ever), the German Gestapo and the Italian political police. Here one may briefly list a few of the most important administrative methods which may be found in all three dictatorships:

(1) Executions without open trial, and wholesale sentencing to concentration camps and places of exile of "counter-revolutionaries," a term that is applied to anyone who is justly or unjustly suspected of harboring critical thoughts about the existing regime. Hitler's "purge" of June 30, 1934, and the execution of 117 persons after the assassination of the Communist leader, Kirov, in November of the same year follow very similar patterns. First the victims are shot. Then there are vague official and semi-official statements, hinting at all sorts of terrorist schemes and treasonable association with agents of foreign powers on the part of the individuals who have conveniently been put out of the way. In Russia there was a second holocaust, a further killing of six-

teen Communists almost two years later, with the whole story of the circumstances of Kirov's assassination conveniently altered to suit the new political needs of the regime.

(2) Treatment of wives and other relatives of political offenders and suspects as hostages. This system was first used on a large scale by the Reds during the Russian civil war, especially with a view to insuring the loyalty of the pre-war officers who had been mobilized for service in the Red Army. It has been imitated in Germany and in Italy and is one of the reasons why accounts of maltreatment in concentration camps by individuals who have escaped are sometimes less specific than they might be otherwise. In the Soviet Union the principle of punishing innocent individuals for the acts of relatives has been formally enacted into the nation's legal code.

Incidentally this practice of treating relatives as hostages goes far to explain some of the amazing and apparently inexplicable abject public confessions in Soviet sabotage and treason trials. A man who might be able to resist any kind of pressure against himself may break down if the future of his family is at stake. Mme. Tchernavina, wife of a well-known Russian scientist, with whom she escaped from a concentration camp in 1931, gives the following interesting first-hand testimony as to the methods which were employed to make her husband confess himself a saboteur:

After my arrest my husband was presented with another alternative: either he must confess his "guilt" or he would be shot, I would get ten years penal servitude and our son be sent to a colony for homeless children.

(3) Making it a grave penal offense for a citizen to leave his country without official permission. One of the greatest marks of distinction between the free and unfree countries of the world is that anyone who is dissatisfied with life in a free country may leave it, unless he is accused of some specific crime. In the unfree countries, especially in the Soviet Union, permission to go abroad is granted suspiciously and reluctantly, and is often denied if the applicant is suspected of holding unsound political views. The most severe penalties, up to and including death, are inflicted on individuals who try to escape by crossing the frontier without benefit of passports. So the dictatorships become vast prison-camps for many of their discontented subjects; escape is a life-and-death adventure.

(4) Finding imaginary scapegoats for the blunders of government. The sabotage trials in the Soviet Union, in one of which two dead men were solemnly indicted for treasonable activities supposedly committed long after their deaths were admirable dress rehearsals for the Reichstag Fire trial. When a leading National Socialist, Herr Rudolf Hess, recently endeavored to make the Jews responsible for all Germany's woes, from the loss of

the World War to the shortage of butter, he was unconsciously following the well trodden path of the many Communist orators who have attributed the sufferings and privations that were an inevitable result of ill conceived and badly executed Soviet agrarian policies to the unfortunate kulaks, long after the last authentic kulak had been effectively liquidated.

The long and impressive list of similarities in psychology and in administrative practice between communism and fascism should not, of course, obscure the existence of important differences between the two systems. In the theoretical field these differences may well seem unbridgeable; it is in the sphere of practice that the many affinities between these anti-democratic and anti-individualistic philosophies become evident.

Russian communism is based on dogmatic faith in the economic doctrines of Karl Marx, as elaborated by Lenin and Stalin. Fascism, both in its German and in its Italian variant, is passionately anti-Marxian. Bolshevism stands for complete expropriation of private owners of the means of production; fascism favors individual, rather than state, operation of most branches of economic life, but imposes many forms of state control and regulation. Bolshevism, in its original, Leninist form, prided itself on its internationalism; fascism extols nationalism above everything. Bolshevism combats every form of religion; Italian fascism upholds respect for Catholicism, as the Italian national faith, while Hitler has pronounced himself in favor of "positive Christianity."

The Russian leaders were, with few exceptions, professional revolutionaries, some of whom had been and some of whom had not been manual workers. But the Bolshevik rank-and-file has always been largely recruited from among manual workers, factory laborers, and miners. Fascism, on the other hand, recruits most of its original adherents from among the middle class, although labor is finally fitted more or less compulsorily into the framework of the fascist state.

Of the three revolutions the Russian has been the most far-reaching and the most destructive. Communism has uprooted more people, violently changed the course of more lives than either Fascism or National Socialism. The German or the Italian is much more apt to be going about his old, pre-revolutionary business, profession, or trade than is the Russian. Lenin and Stalin are responsible for vastly more executions and sentences of imprisonment and banishment than are Mussolini and Hitler. It must, of course, be remembered in this connection that the Soviet regime in Russia was only able to establish its existence firmly after three years of civil war, carried on with the utmost cruelty by both sides, whereas the opposition which Mussolini and Hitler encountered was relatively negligible.

The differences between Fascism and Communism, very great in theory, in many cases shrink appreciably in practice. Stalin's interpretation of Communism, for instance, is becoming steadily and unmistakably more nationalist and Russia-centered. At the present moment German National Socialism is a more explosive force outside of Germany's frontiers than Communism is outside of Russia. National and racial solidarity is a stronger force in actual life than the class solidarity which is preached by Communists. The emotional appeal of National Socialism to Germans outside of Germany—in Austria and Czechoslovakia, in Danzig and Memel—is much more compelling than the appeal of Communism to workers outside of Russia. Both Germany and Italy have given more material help to the Spanish rebels, so far as one can judge from the published reports, than the Soviet Union has given to the "Popular Front" Government, in which Communists are included.

In the religious question also the contrast between the two systems is not so complete as might appear at first sight. Persecution of religion in Russia has indeed been unparalleled in its sweeping and unrelenting character. But both Protestant and Catholic churches in Germany have repeatedly come into sharp conflict with the National Socialist authorities. The grievances of the Evangelical Church are vividly set forth in the following strong terms in a manifesto which was recently read from many pulpits all over Germany:

> The German people is faced with a decision of historic importance. It is whether the Christian faith is to be preserved in Germany, where the Gospel of Christ is being opposed. . . . The Nazi State and Party are employing their power against Christ's Gospel and those who profess it. . . . Those who resist the campaign against the Christian belief must expect to be stigmatized as enemies of the State. This oppression of the conscience, to which is added continual espionage, develops hypocrisy and a vassal mentality, and finally destroys all moral obligations. . . . Many clergy and laymen have suffered for their faith in prison, in concentration camps and by expulsion from their parishes. . . . We must have the right to preach to the German people the faith of their parents. Espionage upon Church work must cease. The ban on religious meetings in public halls must cease. . . .

Now the very fact that this manifesto could be publicly read offers convincing proof that religious persecution is incomparably less severe in Germany than in the Soviet Union. Every grievance that is mentioned exists in considerably aggravated form in Russia. But it would be unthinkable for the remnant of the Russian Orthodox priests, decimated by executions and banishments, to voice any concerted public protest. At the same time the declaration of the German Evangelical pastors shows plainly enough that religious liberty, like every other kind of liberty, fares badly at the hands of a totalitarian state. The supreme devotion of the typical young National Socialist in Germany, of the typical young Fascist in Italy is reserved for secular objects, for the Leader, first of all, and, in a more abstract way, for the ideas of the movement. As for the ideals of obeying God rather than man, of following the dictates of the individual conscience, these are quite incompatible with the nature of any of the post-war dictatorships.

Some people prefer fascism to communism because it has preserved private property. Others regard communism as the superior system because it has destroyed it. If one takes a long-range view it seems doubtful whether this difference between the post-war dictatorial systems, important as it is, will prove of paramount significance. The margin of difference is being narrowed at both ends. Inequality is growing by leaps and bounds in the Soviet Union. There is already a class of high state officials and industrial executives whose earnings exceed those of the ordinary worker in the proportion of ten to one. The spread in wages between the skilled and the unskilled workers is increasing.

A contrary trend toward state regimentation of economic activity and levelling of income is noticeable in Italy and in Germany. It is significant of the long-term tendency of a fascist system that Italy, where Mussolini has ruled for more than fourteen years, as against Hitler's four, has gone much farther than Germany along the way of state control of the banks and basic industries. Yet Germany under the Third Reich is also very far from being a paradise for the private capitalist. As Mr. H. Powys Greenwood remarks:[1]

The process of evolving a new social life will undoubtedly be facilitated by the fact that in Germany to-day differences of income are far less extreme than in many other countries. The inflation was a great leveller. After it had run its course few large fortunes remained. . . . To-day there can be very few men in Germany earning more than £2,000 or £3,000 a year. The return on capital is exceedingly low. The opportunities for making fortunes by speculation are severely curtailed.

So it seems that both utopians who believed that universal equality would prevail under the Soviets and conservatives who hoped that fascism would mean a new lease of life for private capitalism will be disappointed by the actual results in the Soviet Union, Germany, and Italy. The chances are that variations of earnings under the three systems will not be very different. Other contrasts of the early periods of the two systems will also probably be softened with the passing of time. The ruling class of the Soviet Union is becoming steadily less proletarian; the early hostility of the great majority of the Italian and German manual workers to Fascism and National Socialism gives signs of being gradually worn down as a new generation grows up en-

[1] "The German Revolution," p. 171.

tirely under the influence of the dominant system.

Modern historical experience would seem to show that communism can prevail only where, as in Russia, a small wealthy class of industrial magnates and landowners stands face to face with a great mass of poverty-stricken workers and peasants, with only a small, weak middle class as a buffer. Where, as in Germany, the material and educational level was higher, where a much larger part of the population belonged to the middle class and violently resented the idea of being proletarianized, fascism, in some form, was the inevitable outcome of a crisis which submerged democracy.

Whatever may be the differences between fascism and communism, these two new systems of government, with their revised technique of tyranny, certainly represent a unified challenge to the conceptions of democratic government and individual liberty. The challenge is all the more serious because the communist-fascist type of dictatorship, while making itself utterly irresponsible by systematically destroying every agency of individual and group criticism, does attract a genuine measure of popular support, especially among the youth, by means of its high-powered development of the arts of showmanship and propaganda.

Collectivism is written large on the banners of both systems. Advocates of communism and fascism, however much they may disagree on other points, are in substantial agreement on the proposition that liberalism, democracy, individualism are outworn and outmoded, that the salvation of humanity depends on the adoption of their particular brand of collectivist society. How is this theory borne out by the experience of the three great countries which, for varying periods of time, have lived under some form of collectivism?

CHAPTER III

COLLECTIVIST UTOPIA: REALITY AND MIRAGE

IN what now seem to be the safe and tranquil days before the war the idea of a collectivist society was a popular debating theme between utopians and anti-utopians. The former painted alluring pictures of a socialist order where inequalities of wealth would be eliminated and all would work for the common good. The latter predicted that socialism would be followed by a reign of idleness which, in turn, would give way to a rule of despotism. Neither side in these arguments had any blueprints of actual experience to go by. The individualist method was taken for granted in the practical business of daily life.

Now the collectivist state is no longer a fancy. It is very much with us. The issue of individualism and democracy against collectivism and dictatorship is made real and vivid by the existence of the communist and fascist systems in the Soviet Union, Germany, and Italy and by the propaganda of sympathizers with these new creeds in other lands. Both fascism and communism are convinced of their world-conquering mission. Mussolini declares:

Never more than at the present moment have the nations felt such a thirst for an authority, for a direction, for order. If every century has its peculiar doctrine, there are a thousand indications that fascism is that of the present century. Fascism has now attained in the world a universality above all doctrines. Being realized, it represents an epoch in the history of the human mind.

An equal fervor of conviction, somewhat more ponderously expressed, breathes in the following excerpt from the programme adopted by the Sixth Congress of the Communist International, which was framed with Stalin's direct participation and approval:

Imperialism with elemental force uncovers and deepens all the contradictions of capitalist society, brings class oppression to its extreme limit, sharpens to the point of exceptional strain the struggle between capitalist states, makes inevitable imperialistic wars of world dimensions, which shake up the whole system of governing relations and with iron necessity lead to the world revolution of the proletariat.

Such a term as "collectivist state" obviously calls for definition. And one may hope to arrive at such a definition by surveying the very large common denominator of identical administrative practice which may be found in the Soviet Union, Germany, and Italy today.

The collectivist state is omnipotent. It can make and break laws of any description between breakfast and dinner, without worrying about courts and constitutions. It can imprison, exile, expropriate, execute any of its citizens without any nonsense about due process of law or trial by a jury of one's peers.

The collectivist state sets itself up as the supreme arbiter between labor and capital (whether private capital, as in Germany and Italy, or state capital, as in the Soviet Union) in determining wages, hours, and working conditions. In democratic countries the wage-earners, in so far as they are organized, are represented by trade-unions headed by officials of their own choosing. Under collectivism this form of economic democracy goes the way of political democracy. The all-powerful state relieves the workers of the burden of defending their own interests.

The *Arbeitsfront* in Germany, the labor corporation in Italy, the trade-unions in Russia are all controlled and dominated by representatives of the state and the ruling party. Such organizations no doubt transmit and reflect the demands of the workers when state exigencies permit. But the qualification is very important. When "state exigencies" call for higher living costs and lower real wages in Germany, for more intensive work at lower piecework rates in the Soviet Union, for wage-cuts in Italy, the new-style Nazi, Soviet, and Fascist "labor organizations" not only fail to encourage strikes and other expressions of labor discontent but play the rôles of strikebreakers and policemen in checking any such manifestations.

Another feature of the collectivist state is far-reaching interference in what would formerly have been regarded as the sphere of private initiative. Here, of course, the Soviet Union has gone much farther than Germany or Italy. It has wiped out even the smallest "capitalists," such as the peasant with twenty acres of his own land and two cows and the keeper of the dingy village tea room. It has substituted a system under which, in one form or another, the octopus state is not only the banker, manufacturer, and common carrier, but also the baker, the butcher, and the candlestick maker.

But Germany and Italy have gone a considerable distance along the same road of regimenting economic life, even in small details. An Italian business man under the shadow of Mussolini's totalitarian state has little more freedom in managing his own business than the state director of one of the large Soviet industrial trusts. He is heavily taxed; he is limited and directed as to what and how much he may produce and where he is to sell his products. This regimentation has increased since the outbreak of the war with Ethiopia; indeed the organization for war that is such a prominent characteristic of all post-war dictatorships in itself makes for a kind of socialism, for complete subordination of individual to national interest in the ordering of economic life.

The same tendency is visible in Germany, where foreign trade is as closely controlled by the government as it is in Russia. When I was in Germany in 1934 I wanted to sell a piece of jewelry, a personal possession of no great value. I soon gave up the idea when I found that this apparently innocent transaction was probably illegal and meant, in any case, going through an incredible amount of bureaucratic red tape. I was vividly reminded of Russia, where the sale of one's typewriter was in a category with bootlegging operations in America in pre-repeal days.

There can be no mistaking the fact that the collectivist state, where it has been established, has struck deep roots. The number of individuals who have a vested interest in the preservation of the existing regimes in the Soviet Union, Germany, and Italy is considerable. There is the host of newly appointed party and state officials. There is the large part of the youth that naturally falls under the influence of the propaganda slogans of the ruling group when no adverse criticism is tolerated.

The fact that Communist and Fascist Party membership runs through all classes of the population is a tremendous advantage in the matter of keeping in touch with popular sentiment and spying out malcontents. There is small chance for an opposition movement to go far without being detected. The discrepancy between the ideals and the achievements of all three post-war revolutions has indeed brought disillusionment to groups of individuals who were originally enlisted under the red flag, the swastika,

and the fasces. But in the modern collectivist state
the cry of disillusionment is a very still small voice.
It is certain to be quickly and forcibly hushed.

So it is beside the mark to regard either Communism or National Socialism or Fascism as an "experiment," of doubtful stability. All these regimes
must rather be regarded as going concerns, virtually
certain to persist, unless they become involved in unsuccessful wars, and challenging comparison with
democratic governments, both by virtue of their aggressive propaganda and because of their widely
contrasted methods of rule.

The exaggerated and one-sided propaganda em-
anating from Moscow, Berlin, and Rome should not
blind the objective observer to the genuine achievements of the collectivist regimes. The Soviet Union
has made noteworthy strides in industrial development and has created the largest army and possibly
the strongest air force in the world. Hitler has restored to Germany military independence and corresponding political prestige, has covered the country with a network of new motor roads and brought
Germany closer to self-sufficiency in agriculture.
Mussolini has conquered a large colonial empire, re-
claimed land from malarial marshes, built roads and
many other public works.

All three regimes have done a good deal to promote sport and to give the people, especially the
workers, recreation, entertainment, and instruction

through such means as cheap or free vacation outings, reduced tickets for theatres and concerts, organized excursions to museums, art galleries, and places of public interest. When Stalin reviews one of Moscow's monster First of May demonstrations, and Hitler delivers a message of greeting to a great throng of members of his youth organization against the picturesque background of medieval Nuremberg, and Mussolini takes the Fascist salute of cohorts of his Black Shirts in Imperial Rome, each one of these dictators may quite sincerely feel that he has deserved well of his country and that the system which he embodies will some day conquer the world.

Yet one cannot dig far below the surface of any of these dictatorships without realizing that there is more mirage than reality in the idea that the collectivist state is a short cut to a utopian society, free from the familiar weaknesses and defects of democratically governed countries. Highly significant in this connection is the amazing sensitiveness and intolerance which every collectivist state displays at the faintest suggestion of adverse criticism.

If the high-flown claims of unparalleled national achievement and national regeneration which are so constantly and stridently voiced by Stalin, Hitler, Mussolini, and their lieutenants and sublieutenants were founded on fact, one might imagine that the dictators would positively welcome public criticism, merely for the pleasure of bowling it over by exposing its weaknesses. One could fancy the Soviet Government promoting coast-to-coast speaking tours by opponents of such varied views as Grand Duke Cyril and Leon Trotzky, Mussolini inviting Professor Salvemini to resume his old chair at an Italian university and to debate freely with Fascist spokesmen on economics and finance, Hitler issuing similar invitations to émigré German Social Democrats and Communists. Alas, nothing of the kind is within the realm of remote possibility. Nothing is more eloquently suggestive of the real state of affairs under the dictatorships than the extraordinary nervous care which is taken to prevent the least breath of criticism from reaching their subjects. Regimes that have built up huge standing armies and police forces fly into a mixture of rage and panic if they discover that a few copies of some critical pamphlet have been smuggled across their frontiers, that a few of their subjects have been secretly meeting for free discussion. In order to prevent such developments they resort to the most subtle espionage, to the most brutal terrorism. This incontestable fact, equally applicable to the Soviet Union, Germany, and Italy, scarcely fits in with the pleasant pictures, so zealously painted by the propaganda agencies, of happy, contented, united peoples, marching to ever greater heights of material and cultural achievement under the banners of their beloved leaders.

The effect of the muzzle which every dictatorship

clamps on its people was vividly brought home to me when I left Moscow for a trip to America in the winter of 1932–1933, returning to the Soviet Union in the spring of 1933. Making every allowance for the traditionally higher American standard of living, there seemed to me not the slightest room for doubt that Russia relatively, as well as absolutely, was in a vastly worse plight than the United States. In other words, the Russian, looking back to 1913, had more cause for complaint than the American, making the same retrospective comparison.

The American farm crisis was at its height. But farmers in Iowa and North Dakota were not dying in immense numbers of sheer starvation, like peasants in Ukraina and the North Caucasus. Unemployment in the United States had reached formidable and unprecedented figures. But when, after returning to Moscow, I read off to Russian friends a list of the foodstuffs that were given to the unemployed in Milwaukee as part of their relief, they exclaimed in incredulity that no employed Soviet worker could hope for such quantity and variety of food, that the list sounded like the ration of a highly placed Soviet official.

Yet I found many people in America convinced that the Soviet Union was triumphantly forging ahead, while America was sinking into some unpredictable catastrophe. The main reason for what seemed to me this complete lack of any sense of proportion in comparing the state of the two countries was that America's troubles stared from every newspaper and magazine headline, while Russia's were carefully concealed by an all-embracing censorship. There was plenty of publicity for the debt-ridden farmers of the Middle West, not a word for the starving peasants of southern and southeastern Russia. The sufferings of the American unemployed were mirrored in hundreds of books and thousands of articles. One could search the files of the Soviet press in vain for even a single description of the sufferings of Russia's compulsorily employed exiles in timber camps and new construction enterprises, housed in foul barracks and dugouts, often under arctic conditions, receiving as "pay" barely enough food to make it physically possible for them to perform their allotted tasks.

This same unequal condition prevails in the matter of reporting democratic countries for dictatorships and dictatorships for democratic countries. No Soviet correspondent in Washington or London could conceivably draw a contrast between the results of private and state operation of industry and agriculture, favorable to the former, and either have it published in his newspaper or hope to hold his job after having written it. Neither could any Fascist journalist in these capitals suggest, by the remotest implication, that democracy in some ways might be superior to dictatorship. But any American or British "friend of the Soviet Union," "friend of the New Germany," or admirer of Mussolini can write and publish, without the least difficulty, the most extravagant, unqualified praises of the collectivist regimes, drawing any comparisons he likes between communist (or fascist) alleged achievements, discipline and self-sacrifice and capitalistic (or democratic) supposed breakdown, weakness, and general inefficiency.

On the other hand the journalist in Moscow, Berlin, or Rome whose attitude toward the existing regime stops short of complete acquiescence or enthusiasm finds his pathway a thorny one. His telegrams are censored; his mail is tampered with; he soon becomes conscious of official discrimination; and, if he fails to mend his ways, expulsion from the country or, what amounts to the same thing, refusal of permission to return to it, is likely to be his ultimate fate. While a dictatorship cannot, of course, employ against a correspondent of foreign nationality the extreme means of pressure and regimentation which it uses against its own subjects, it can over a period of time usually succeed in eliminating, by direct or indirect means, its more outspoken critics in the foreign press corps, while, of course, cherishing its friends and admirers.

Moreover, it is far easier to make out, with impressive documentation, a case, even an exaggerated case, against the weaknesses of democracy than to frame a similar indictment of the modern-style dictatorship. The faults of democracy are shouted from the housetops; the crimes of dictatorship, in the overwhelming majority of cases, are committed behind doors that are not only closed, but carefully barred and bolted. The most damaging facts about the effects of the world economic crisis can be extracted from the official governmental reports of democratic countries. For the details of the hunger in the towns and the famine in the country districts that were the accompaniment of Russia's rapid industrialization after 1929 one is largely dependent on the testimony of a few foreign eyewitnesses who were not concerned with the possibility of being refused a Soviet return visa.

Yet, as Lenin once remarked, "facts are stubborn things," no matter how they may be twisted and distorted and reshaped in the dictatorial propaganda mills. Despite the tremendous advantage which the collectivist state enjoys over the democracy in suppressing and concealing the less pleasant features of its existence, there is an overwhelming body of factual evidence to show that, wherever comparison is possible, democracy has nothing to fear and everything to gain from a full and frank comparison of its record with that of dictatorship.

I advisedly insert the qualifying phrase "wherever comparison is possible," because behind each of the three major experiments in the collectivist state there is an element of fanatical enthusiasm which it is difficult, if not impossible, to measure accurately. Who can say how much satisfaction the Russian, or German, or Italian, especially of the younger generation, derives from the mere fact of marching in step with a great mass movement, taking part in huge parades and demonstrations, joining in the singing of the "Internationale" or the "Horst-Wessel Lied" or the "Giovinezza"?

On the other hand democratic peoples also have their intangible values, their cherished traditions, even if they have not developed the technique of mass regimentation and mass showmanship that is so characteristic of the new-style dictatorship. The faith of Lincoln's Gettysburg Speech to the American, the spirit of the revolutionary slogan "Liberty, Equality, Fraternity" to the Frenchman, the Englishman's consciousness that his country's history from the Barons at Runnymede down through John Hampden to the great theorist of liberty, John Stuart Mill, and beyond has been identified with a process of ever widening freedom: such things are apt to weigh quite as heavily in the balance in periods of national crisis as the newer creeds of communism and fascism.

In the more easily defined, material things of life the comparison between the democracies and the dictatorships is invariably on balance, if not in every detail, in favor of the former. Take at random five countries of varied racial composition and historical background, which are, however, united by the bond of common democratic institutions: the United States, Great Britain, Canada, Sweden, and Switzerland. Take also at random five other countries which have gone the way of dictatorship: the Soviet Union, Germany, Italy, Poland, and Yugoslavia. Is there any doubt which group gives its people more and better food, higher real wages, more reasonable and equitable taxation, more security against arbitrary arrest and imprisonment, more liberty for the individual to follow his own bent in life, free from military and industrial and thought conscription?

Contrary to the poetic line about the rich becoming richer and the poor poorer, and the gloomy prediction of Karl Marx that the development of the capitalist system would lead to greater concentration of wealth at one end of the social scale and greater poverty at the other, experience shows that under the modern industrial system a nation's material well-being is pretty faithfully reflected in the condition of all classes of the population. Where there are most millionaires there are also the largest number of workers owning automobiles and homes, and farmers whose houses are provided with telephones and modern plumbing. Where the masses have a low standard of living the wealth of the well-to-do classes is much more circumscribed. So a comparison of real wages is a fair comparison of national well-being.

The International Labor Office of the League of
Nations made a report on real wages in July, 1930.
Of eight of the countries covered, four democracies
and four dictatorships, every one of the democracies
was in the higher brackets, every one of the dictatorships in the lower. Here are the precise figures:

United States	190	Poland	61
Canada	155	Yugoslavia	45
Great Britain	100	Spain	40
The Netherlands	82	Italy	39

It may be argued that the form of government is
not decisive in determining national well-being,
that such factors as natural wealth, geographical
location and course of historical development must
be taken into consideration. While it is certainly true
that no governmental system can altogether offset
extreme poverty in natural resources, the connection between free institutions and a relatively high
standard of living in such matters as food, housing,
means of communication, and material conveniences
is surely too general to be accidental. The disinte-
gration of the vast rich Spanish Empire, as contrasted
with the preservation of the British, is an illustration
of the fact that freedom is a better guaranty than
autocracy of the flexibility and resourcefulness that
go with stable empire building.

I recall a discussion which I once had with an eminent Chinese scholar who maintained that political
democracy and individual liberty, while highly de-

sirable, were something in the nature of luxuries which wealthy and secure nations could afford. Nations that were less fortunately situated, that were carrying on a hard struggle for existence under conditions of great poverty, must, he argued, seek sterner forms of administration, with more authoritarian leadership. In this proposition he saw an explanation if not a justification of communism and fascism.

My own contention, which was unchanged by the able arguments of my Chinese acquaintance, was that free institutions are not a kind of luxury appendage which nations can take on after reaching a certain stage of material prosperity, but a vitally important instrument for achieving this stage. In other words, peoples do not become free after they have become prosperous; they become prosperous in no small measure as a result of being free.

The whole course of development in the three post-war collectivist states bears out this theory. The state, which Nietzsche once appropriately characterized as "the coldest of all cold monsters," has exploited the people under the rule of the dictators to an extent which would be impossible under democracy. The course of events under all three collectivist regimes is full of practical illustrations of how, under dictatorship, the immediate comfort and welfare of the people are certain to be sacrificed for the sake of vaulting military ambitions and doctrinaire schemes of economic reconstruction which are supposed to benefit future generations. The universal hunger (from which only highly placed bureaucrats, favored groups of executives, and especially skilled workers were spared) which accompanied the first Russian Five Year Plan, and which deepened into widespread famine in 1932–1933, is the most vivid example in this connection. But the sporadic shortages in Germany of butter, eggs, pork, and other foodstuffs (unknown under the much abused republican regime which preceded Hitler) and the persistent downward trend of real wages and upward trend of taxation in Italy under Mussolini also show that the collectivist state, either in its communist or in its fascist form, is emphatically not calculated to promote the general welfare of its subjects.

The reasons why dictatorships, unlike democracies, are so prone to exact the last ounce of suffering and privation from the people under their rule are deeply imbedded in the nature of the two systems. Consider the enormous difference in psychology between a Stalin, a Hitler, a Mussolini, and an American President or a British or French Premier. The dictator is as absolute as a Roman Emperor. He need only render an accounting of his policies to packed Party congresses or national assemblies, the members of which have been hand-picked to the last degree. He can only be removed by assassination or rebellion; and rebellion against the modern totalitarian state, with its high-powered combination of propaganda and terrorism, may be ruled out as virtually impracticable, at least in time of peace.

The leader of a democratic government, on the other hand, must submit the case for his administration to free elections of the whole body of his countrymen at stated intervals. His every act receives, along with the praise of his supporters, the criticism of his opponents, freely expressed in newspapers, public meetings, and statements. The individuals or newspapers which have supported him in the earlier stages of his administration may change their attitude if he adopts policies which seem to be inconsistent with his original promises.

It is not difficult to imagine which type of ruler is more apt to launch policies that will impose immense suffering and deprivation on the masses of the people for the sake of some hypothetical future good—the irremovable dictator, responsible only to himself, or the democratic leader who has been selected and may be removed by the free suffrage of his fellow citizens. Of course no head of a government rules in an absolute vacuum. Russia's Tsars, with the exception of a few who were hopelessly feebleminded, endeavored, according to their lights, to promote the welfare of their subjects and the economic prosperity of the country. The modern dictator has his numerous agencies of espionage, his sources of information about the prevalent mood among various classes of his subjects. There is no doubt an extreme limit beyond which neither Stalin nor Hitler nor Mussolini would venture to test the endurance of the Russian, German, or Italian people. But that extreme limit represents a far lower abyss of poverty and deprivation than any democratic state has ever touched.

All the collectivist states are aggressively propagandist in spirit. All of them love to paint in their gagged and controlled press, with no possibility of argument or criticism, highly imaginary contrasts between the happiness and well-being which their regimes have produced and the misery and despair which are supposed to prevail everywhere else. The Soviet press has specialized in drawing up parallel columns headed "With Them" and "With Us"—the first a record of unrelieved gloom in the capitalist world, the second a chronicle of unqualified good cheer in the Soviet Union. An interesting check-up on this contrast is an objective comparison, based respectively on American and Soviet official figures as regards wages and prices, of the food supply of American and Soviet workers.

A recent Soviet statistical estimate gives the average monthly wage of all workers and employees for 1935 as 190 rubles. What this implies in terms of staple foodstuffs, and how it compares with American wage-scales, are revealed by the following table. The American worker's average income is com-

puted at seventy dollars a month, according to the
United States Bureau of Labor statistics for 1933:

Commodity	Russian Scale [1]	American Scale
Pounds of butter	19	240
Pounds of sausage	30	176
Pounds of sugar	90	1,120
Pounds of second-grade beef	63	280
Pounds of first-grade beef	40	200

In other words, the American worker's wage, in
terms of real food values, in one of the worst years
of an unprecedented depression, was from five to
twelve times the Soviet worker-employee's wage in
1935, when there had been some improvement in conditions by comparison with the bleak starvation and
semi-starvation standards of 1932 and 1933. Of
course neither the American nor the Russian worker
could afford to spend a month's wages on a single
foodstuff. But the discrepancy between what an individualist system, at its worst, could supply to
American workers and what a collectivist system, up
to date, could supply to Russians would not be diminished if one undertook a broad survey of comparative
household budgets, instead of restricting the comparison to a few commodities. A long list of inexpensive
articles of daily use in America, from bananas to
toilet paper and from nails to chocolate, either are

[1] The purchasing power of Russian wages is calculated on the basis
of official Soviet food prices, as reported in the Moscow *Daily News* after
the abolition of rationing, in September, 1935.

unobtainable in Russia or can be bought only with great difficulty and at fabulous prices.

If it were not for the extravagant claims of official Soviet propaganda (*e.g.*, the repeated assertion that the Soviet Union has "abolished poverty") and for the tall tales set in circulation by some returned tourists and stay-at-home enthusiasts for the Soviet Union, it would scarcely be necessary to labor the point that the American standard of living, even during the most severe crisis of half a century, remained vastly superior to the Russian. That the Russians themselves have a pretty shrewd suspicion of this fact, despite the strenuous propaganda efforts of the Soviet Government's kept press, is evident from the following "anecdote," or satirical joke, about a Russian who tells a friend that, according to the official programme, the Soviet Union will "overtake and outstrip" America, as the leading capitalist country. "Just let me off when we come abreast of America: I don't want to go any farther," is the retort of the second Russian.

What is more important, in evaluating the achievements of the Soviet brand of collectivist state, is that the Russian people, if one may accept the plain evidence of Soviet statistics, are worse fed than they were two decades ago under Tsarism. While the grain crop of 1935 was well above those of 1931 and 1932, which were an immediate prelude to famine, the *per capita* grain yield of 1913 was not quite attained. The Moscow correspondent of the "Christian Science Monitor," citing Stalin as authority for the 1935 figure, writes as follows on this point:

The Russian grain yield in 1935 was about 91,600,000 metric tons, as compared with 76,000,000 metric tons in 1913. But the population of Soviet Russia in 1935, according to Soviet official estimates, was 171,000,000, as compared with 138,000,000 for this same territory in 1913.

So, although 1935 gave the best harvest since the Revolution, it still fell a little short of the 1913 *per capita* yield of pre-war Russia, which communist sympathizers like to depict as incredibly backward, if not downright barbarous. Much greater has been the impoverishment of Russian agriculture in livestock, with the corresponding inevitable deterioration in the supply of meat, milk, and dairy products. A prominent Communist agricultural expert, Y. A. Yakovlev, published the following comparative livestock figures in "Izvestia" (official organ of the Soviet Government) of February 21, 1936:

	1916	1935
Horses	35,100,000	15,900,000
Large horned cattle	58,900,000	49,200,000
Sheep and goats	115,200,000	61,000,000
Pigs	20,300,000	22,500,000

Here one has in a nutshell the explanation of the Soviet food prices, which are abnormally high in relation to the earnings of the workers and employees, and also the proof that Russians, by and large, are eating less and worse than before the Revolution. There has certainly been no importation of foreign foodstuffs to make up for the heavy loss of meat, milk, and fats, because foreign exchange, under the state monopoly of foreign trade, has been closely rationed and reserved almost entirely for the purchase of machinery and essential raw materials. Some individual groups of the Russian population may have gained at the expense of others. But the national food balance is clearly less favorable than it was before the war. The food situation seems likely to deteriorate further as a result of the drought which affected a considerable part of European Russia in 1936, and which had already led, in the summer of 1936, to such unfavorable developments as wholesale slaughtering of cattle and acute shortage of fresh vegetables and fruits.

Valuable information on the material position of the Soviet worker is to be found in Sir Walter Citrine's book, "I Search for Truth in Russia," a summary of the author's impressions during a trip to the main cities and industrial centres of the Soviet Union in the autumn of 1935. Unlike some socialist intellectuals who have visited the Soviet Union Sir Walter, himself an ex-worker and Secretary of the British Trade-Union Congress was interested in the Russian worker as a human being, not as a part of an abstract class; and his work is consequently full of the concrete practical information about wages, housing, and general living conditions that is often sadly lacking in the more theoretical books about communism. Sir Walter, after carefully checking the prices of Soviet foodstuffs and manufactured goods with those of Great Britain and France, reached the conclusion that the purchasing power of the Soviet ruble was about threepence, or six cents. So the purchasing power of the monthly average wage of the Soviet worker or employee works out at less than twelve American dollars. Before the war the monthly wage of the Russian manual worker (not counting the employees, who were somewhat more highly paid) was twenty-five or thirty rubles, nominally twelve and a half or fifteen dollars. But, as the cost of living in pre-war Russia was very low, the purchasing power of the ruble, as regards food and clothing, was more than its exchange equivalent of a little over fifty American cents; the real wage of the Russian worker was probably equal to eighteen or twenty dollars a month.

Another investigator of Soviet financial conditions, Mr. L. E. Hubbard, after a careful study of present and pre-war Russian wages and prices, arrives at the following conclusion: [2]

It would probably be not far from the facts to put the puchasing power of the rouble in 1936 in respect of the most important articles of consumption at one-sixteenth of the 1913 rouble, or, taking into consideration housing rents, travelling, etc., at one-twelfth of the 1913 rouble.

[2] "Soviet Money and Finance" (Macmillan, 1936), p. 332.

Money wages, as has been pointed out, are approximately seven times the 1913 level, so that the decline in real wages for the proletariat, the supposed ruling class in the Soviet Union, from the exceptionally low level of Tsarist times has been appreciable. Mr. Hubbard also states that "the average Russian can buy with his week's wages about as much food as the Londoner can buy with nine shillings," another of the many indications that the standard of the majority of the Russian workers is that of the unemployed, rather than of the employed, in Great Britain and the United States.

Since the peasants, who comprise about three-fourths of the Soviet population, far outnumber the city workers, conditions in the rural districts afford a fairer barometer of Soviet achievement than conditions in the towns. The ordeal through which the peasants passed between 1929 and 1933, the period of compulsory changing over from individual to collective farming, is without precedent in any other European country. Millions perished of outright hunger and the diseases, such as typhus and influenza, that follow in the wake of hunger, during the great famine of 1932–1933, which was brought on by ruthless requisitions and colossal blunders in the administration of the collective farming system. Millions more, the so-called kulaks, with their families, were driven from their homes and, in many cases, were packed off to concentration camps where labor was hard, food scanty, and mortality rates, especially among the weak and old, frightfully high.

Since the low point of 1933 there has been a turn for the better in Soviet agriculture. The peasants have resigned themselves to the state landlordism of collective farming, just as their ancestors, after futile revolts, resigned themselves to serfdom. There has been no convincing evidence of famine since 1933, although the full effect of the drought of 1936 cannot be measured at the time of writing.

But recovery from the famine level of 1933 can proceed a considerable distance without approaching the very modest pre-war normal level of well-being. With the best of climatic luck and the smoothest working discipline it would be impossible for peasants who were down to stark famine in 1933 to reach a very abundant stage of prosperity by 1937. Heavy taxes in kind must be paid to the state, a circumstance that limits the peasant's capacity for earning and accumulation.

The peasants who rose a little above the general poverty line have been "liquidated" as kulaks, and the Soviet village today presents an unrelieved picture of drab and dingy poverty. If there is a peasant in the Soviet Union who possesses an automobile, a telephone in his house, or a bathroom with modern sanitation, I failed to meet him during many years of extensive travel in Russia. The world's prize for cynicism might well go to Karl Radek (recently sentenced to ten years of imprisonment because of suspected complicity in one of the mysterious plots that are always allegedly cropping up against Stalin) for assuring the French political leader M. Herriot, during the latter's trip to the Soviet Union in the famine year, 1933, that the future of Russia's forcibly collectivized peasants was far brighter than that of America's Middle Western farmers. If the standard of living of the Russian worker resembles that of the unemployed in America and Western Europe, the status of the peasant, as regards food, housing, and clothing, is comparable with that of the poor sharecropper. Indeed the economic position of the whole Russian peasantry is that of share-croppers, with an all-powerful state as landlord, telling them what and how much they must plant, how much they must deliver to the towns, how much they may keep, what they shall receive for their labor.

So much for the record of Russian Communism, the most complete form of the collectivist state, in changing the material condition of the two classes in whose name the Bolshevik Revolution was made, the industrial workers and the peasants. Similar disillusioning results are to be found if one examines the records of German National Socialism and Italian Fascism not under the bright glare of parade speeches by Hitler and Mussolini, but under the cold clear light of objective facts.

It is true that Germany and Italy have not suffered, like Russia, from large-scale destruction of
national wealth. The two fascist revolutions took
place with relatively little opposition; the tremendous reconstruction bill which was entailed by the
prolonged Russian civil war, with its havoc and
devastation by both sides, was avoided. Moreover,
neither Hitler nor Mussolini has adopted measures
calculated to make the peasants under his rule slaughter their cattle on an enormous scale, as the Russian
peasants did under the stimulus of the forced social-
ization of their property. Nevertheless the balance-
sheet of National Socialism and of Fascism in terms
of individual welfare is clearly negative.

Addressing his spectacular Party Congress at Nuremberg, Hitler last September drew up an impressive list of achievements which he claimed for his
regime: five million unemployed put back to work,
automobile output increased fivefold, thousands of
miles of new roads laid, hundreds of thousands of
new houses built. Stalin and Mussolini could draw
up equally striking lists of construction works, carried out under their rule, which, to audiences of
spellbound followers, might seem overwhelming evidence of the superiority of the respective dictator's
particular type of regime.

There are, however, two basic objections to this
kind of *ex parte* statement, which the propaganda
agencies of the collectivist regimes turn out so easily,

without fear of criticism or contradiction within their own borders. In the first place, there is no comparative consideration of the industrial and economic achievements of those peoples which have retained free institutions. A most misleading impression is often conveyed by the fact that democratic countries take it more or less as a matter of course that new factories and power plants should be erected, that motor and rail transport should constantly adopt new technical improvements, that new roads and huge bridges should be built. Under all the new collectivist regimes, on the other hand, any piece of noteworthy construction is greeted with a chorus of shrill ballyhoo as something unprecedented, unique, and attributable to the unparalleled genius of the *Vozhd*, *Führer*, or *Duce* and the special merits of his system. Boulder Dam, for instance, is a far bigger and more significant engineering achievement than Russia's Dnieprostroi; but it has probably not received a tenth part of the lavish publicity which was accorded to the Soviet enterprise.

A second criticism which would apply both to Hitler's Nuremberg speech and to the many similar declarations by Stalin and Mussolini is that all negative facts are carefully omitted, although the value of many communist and fascist public works and other enterprises cannot be fairly assessed without some consideration of the cost, human and material, of their construction. Hitler's record of achievement as stated without qualification is one thing. Hitler's record, examined in the double perspective of the constructive accomplishments of the democratic regime which preceded him and of the sacrifices and deprivations, past and prospective, which he has imposed on the masses of the German people is something very different.

Hitler boasted of "640,000 tons of shipping under construction at German wharves in 1936." Under the Weimar Republic, which the dictator likes to depict as one of utter impotence and futility, the tonnage of German shipping, which was practically wiped out at the end of the war had reached 3,768,-000 tons by January 1, 1928. In other words, the amount of annual construction had averaged around 400,000 tons during a period which, in its first years, was characterized by the greatest economic difficulties in the shape of post-war rioting and sporadic outbreaks of civil war, together with destructive inflation. Hitler spoke of "tremendous new homestead colonies, with hundreds of thousands of houses." The Weimar Republic existed for a longer time than Hitler; but it could count the new houses which were built under its rule not in hundreds of thousands, but in millions. Between 1919 and 1933 approximately three million new dwellings were erected.

Germany before the war was internationally famous for its high level of scientific attainment (at that time no distinction was made between "Aryan" and "non-Aryan" German scientists), for the efficiency of its business leaders, and for the skill and assiduity of its workers. These great assets in creating national wealth remained constant through the three regimes of modern Germany: the Imperial system, which came to an end with the loss of the World War, the democratic Republic, and the National Socialist Third Reich. Hitler and the National Socialist Party emphatically did not create these assets, and it is difficult to see how such National Socialist measures as the wholesale exclusion of Jews from scientific and administrative posts, regardless of individual merit, or the reduction in the number of university students can add to them.

Hitler's claims of achievement shrink further in perspective if one considers the sacrifices at which they have been purchased. There has been a definite fall in the national standard of living; the queues for butter and eggs and meat which were hitherto the special characteristic of the Soviet regime have now made their appearance in Berlin and other German cities. While nominal wage rates have shown little change since Hitler came into power the working class has been hit in two ways, by an increased cost of living and by an increase in the number of compulsory and semi-compulsory levies on wages in the form of contributions for National Socialist Party and other public purposes. A careful and reliable foreign estimate [3] indicates that the cost of living has risen by 15 or 20 per cent, while the pamphlet "Labor Under Hitler," [4] cites figures taken from the investigations of the German Labor Front to show that the average industrial wage was reduced from 26 marks a week to 22 marks by "taxes, insurances, dues and other contributions."

That the putting to work of five million unemployed has been brought about not by absorption into industry at normal rates of pay, but rather by artificial devices—such as the institution of compulsory labor service at virtually no pay for youths, enlistment in the Army, sending of large numbers of young people to work on the land (again for practically no pay except board and keep), dismissals of women from employment, and clearing of the public services of Jews and persons who were considered politically undesirable—is evident from the fact that Germany's wage and salary earners received two billion more marks in 1931, a year of severe depression, than in 1935. [5]

The reëmployment and the industrial revival which have occurred since Hitler came into power rest on the dubious base of an intensive programme

[3] *Cf.* the report on economic conditions in Germany by Mr. E. C. Donaldson Rawlins, commercial counsellor of the British Embassy in Berlin, published by the Department of Overseas Trade of the British Government.

[4] *Cf.* the article by Mr. Norman Thomas, in "Foreign Affairs" for April, 1936.

[5] *Cf.* despatch from Berlin on the financial page of the "Christian Science Monitor" for September 4, 1936.

of rearmament. In order to drive ahead this programme both the food needs of the country and the service of its foreign debts have been sacrificed; Hitler has resorted to the Bolshevik financial expedient of stopping payments on the financial obligations of the preceding regime. The manufacture of cannon, airplanes, tanks, shells, and other weapons of modern warfare creates employment; but it is totally unproductive. Armaments can only destroy: they can never create material values. The full extent of the German national sacrifice for rearmament cannot be measured, because it is impossible to obtain full and precise figures of the budget and the internal debt in the Third Reich. But the occasional spectacular displays of armed strength speak for themselves.

Not only is intensive armament a thoroughly unproductive way of solving the unemployment problem; it is also necessarily temporary. Restrained for almost fifteen years by the disarmament provisions of the Treaty of Versailles, Germany had a good deal of ground to make up during the first years of its rearmament. But Hitler himself recognizes that a time will come in the fairly near future when other occupation must be found for many of the workers now employed in munitions factories. In his Nuremberg speech he suggested that substitute occupation could be found in the "great German raw material industry" which he envisages as arising "through our chemistry, machine, and mining industries."

Taken in conjunction with other parts of the speech and with the pronounced trend in Germany under National Socialism toward autarchy, or maximum self-dependence as regards essential raw materials, this seems to foreshadow a huge investment, probably with considerable state support in the form of subsidies, in the artificial production of the raw materials which Germany lacks, in the making of synthetic rubber, for instance, in the distillation of oil from coal and the use of woodpulp fibre as a substitute for wool and cotton. Previous experience has indicated that the manufacture of such substitute raw materials, while it may be scientifically feasible, is commercially disadvantageous, because of the high costs of production, and also leaves much to be desired in the matter of quality. So the probable economic consequences of a plunge into production of this kind seem dubious, to say the least. Konrad Heiden, one of the most objective critics of National Socialism, once observed: "The National Socialist state of the future rests upon general poverty, relieved by enthusiasm and maintained by terrorization."

The perspectives held out by Hitler's speech do not seem to weaken the force of this prediction, which, incidentally, seems to apply equally well to Italy and to the Soviet Union.

What of the record of the third "collectivist utopia," Mussolini's Fascist state in Italy? Economically, it is strikingly similar to that of the Third Reich. On one side of the ledger one sees grandiloquent claims and boasts by the leader, a genuine generation of enthusiasm among a part of the population, especially among the youth, an enhancement of external discipline and smartness in bearing, calculated to impress the casual foreign visitor, substantial public works, notably in hydroelectric power development, road building, and land reclamation. On the other side, wages that are so low that they can scarcely be reduced further, and taxes so high that they can scarcely be increased further. While the Soviet Union, Germany, and Italy differ widely in geographical and historical background and in the economic problems which confront them, one verdict does seem to hold good for all three collectivist dictatorships. All of them make their peoples pay vastly more in suffering and deprivation for such measure of economic progress as they achieve than any democratic regime has ever done.

Mussolini's economic policy during the first part of his regime was marked by ruthless deflation. Repeated wage and salary cuts were supposed to be accompanied by corresponding reductions in the cost of living. The first part of this programme, however, was fulfilled much more effectively than the second; if one accepts the authority of the League of Nations' *Bulletin mensuel de statistique*, for February, 1933, wages were reduced between 40 and 50 per cent between 1923 and 1932, while the cost of living declined only 5 per cent. There is abundant evidence from Fascist sources both of the severity of the wage-cuts and of the difficulty of bringing about parallel reductions in the cost of living. While the wage-earning and salaried classes have thus seen their standards of living cut down, a steadily increasing burden of taxation has been pressing on the more well-to-do classes. The pre-war Italian Government took 13 per cent of the national income in taxation in 1914; as early as 1925 the proportion had reached 20 per cent, and the tendency since that time has been toward further increases. The Italians have paid heavily for the upkeep of the Black Shirt Militia, for the country's expanded military budget, for the huge supplementary police and spy system and other necessary attributes of the collectivist state.

The principle of fascism is sometimes defended on the ground that a single absolute leader, invested with full authority and responsibility, can act with more speed and resolution than the head of a parliamentary regime. Such a theory would be more tenable if there were any guaranty of a dictator's infallibility. When the dictator blunders there is no corrective; and many of Italy's difficulties can be traced directly to mistakes of Mussolini. The decision to stabilize the lira at a higher gold value than the French franc was one such mistake; it had a crippling effect on Italian foreign trade and helped to make necessary the internal policy of ruthless deflation which persisted until the war in Ethiopia.

For an overpopulated country like Italy, Mussolini's insistence on a high birth rate and discouragement of emigration were scarcely advisable measures; the Italian dictator finally believed himself obliged to take the method of relieving population pressure which historical experience has shown to be least hopeful: that of colonial expansion. The cheap victory which poison gas, airplanes, and other modern weapons made possible for the invading Italian armies over the ill armed, untrained tribal levies of Ethiopia may temporarily raise Mussolini's prestige at home. But on any long-range view it seems likely to aggravate rather than to solve Italy's economic and social problems.

What material benefits can Italy expect from the possession of Ethiopia? Trade? An outlet for surplus population? Valuable minerals and raw materials?

As regards trade, Ethiopia's total imports in 1934 were valued at $4,523,000. A minimum estimate of Italy's war cost, which is by no means ended, is $800,000,000. Some estimates place it at almost a billion dollars. If we take the lower figure and reckon interest charges at 5 per cent, it is evident that a monopoly of the Ethiopian market would pay little more than 10 per cent of the annual interest charge on Italy's war outlay. So far as colonization is concerned, much of the large expanse of Ethiopia that appears on maps consists of uninhabitable deserts and wild mountain ranges and gorges. Italian settlement, even in the more fertile regions, is certain to be difficult for many years because of the guerilla warfare against the Italian occupation. The experience of the French and the Spaniards in Morocco and of the Japanese in Manchuria indicates that, while a primitive people cannot successfully stand up to a modern army in open fight, it can carry on annoying partisan warfare over long periods of time wherever natural conditions, in the form of mountains, forests, and other natural refuges, are favorable. It is noteworthy that only 52,-419 Italians resided in African colonies in 1931, although Italy has been a colonial power for forty years. Ethiopia's wealth in natural resources is highly debatable; and in any case years of costly railway and other development would be necessary before they could be developed.

Advocates of the collectivist systems have their negative as well as their positive arguments. They like to represent their regimes as the sole alternatives to something much worse. Impressionable and sympathetic visitors to Russia, when they stumble on a filthy hospital or an overcrowded, unsanitary railway station, or some other stark evidence of poverty and neglect, are reassured on being told that every defect in the Soviet system is largely attributable to the incredibly backward state of Russia before the Revolution. The same type of visitor in Germany or Italy, if he finds anything amiss, is told that such minor criticisms should not weigh in the balance when one considers that Hitler and Mussolini saved their countries from Bolshevism.

These stock explanations are as one-sided and unconvincing as the claims of the dictators about the "unparalleled," "unsurpassed" constructive achievements of their regimes, if they are examined in the light of ascertainable historical facts. Consider first the condition of pre-war Russia. Obviously there were grave weaknesses and defects in any system which, when overthrown, left the field free for such a sweeping and destructive social revolution as that of Bolshevism. There were bad slum conditions in the towns, and there was much poverty in the rural districts. Contrasts of wealth and poverty, with the consequent incitement to class hatred, were greater than in most countries.

But the country was very far from being the howling wilderness, culturally and economically, that Soviet apologists customarily take for granted. Russia's pre-war contributions to literature, drama, and music ranked high in the international scale and certainly compare favorably with those of Soviet artists, hampered as they are at every turn by the demand that art must be "on the class front." The bad conditions were not stagnant and permanent; illiteracy was steadily decreasing; a strong coöperative movement was developing among the peasants, especially in Siberia; in the decade before the war, wages and standards of living were rising. Because it was a new country with a vast expanse of territory, Russia's industrial development proceeded rapidly; there were periods before the war when the annual gains in industrial output and railway construction were as great as in the period of strained industrial advance marked by the first Soviet Five Year Plan. Finally it is engineers, scientists, physicians, trained in the universities and schools of old Russia, rather than inexperienced Young Communists and hardboiled Gay-Pay-Oo drivers of forced labor and "discoverers" of dubious sabotage plots who deserve most of the credit for such advance in industry and social services as the Soviet Union may fairly claim. If the cruelties of the Soviet regime have their parallels and to some extent their origins in the administrative practices of the Romanov autocracy, the creative achievements of that regime would be unthinkable if the pre-war Russian educated class had not, in many fields, achieved high standards of culture and intellectual training.

What of the claim that Hitler and Mussolini saved Italy and Germany from Bolshevism? If it were true it would be an important mitigating factor in judging the severities of the fascist states. For neither of these has destroyed human life and inflicted other forms of suffering on anything like the Russian Bolshevik scale, and there is no reason to suppose that communism, had it gained the upper hand in Italy or Germany, would have been any less ruthless. But, while hypothetical judgments are always debatable, there is strong reason for believing that the claim is not true, in the case of either dictator.

In the case of Italy, Mussolini himself has testified that the danger of Bolshevism had passed long before the Fascist march on Rome. For he wrote in his newspaper, "Popolo d'Italia," of July 2, 1921:

> To say that a Bolshevik danger still exists in Italy means taking base fears for reality. Bolshevism is overthrown.

This statement seems to correspond with reality. The revolutionary tide was clearly ebbing. The fiasco with the occupation of the factories in 1920, the split in the labor ranks between Communists and Socialists, the nation-wide weariness of constant strikes and interruptions of normal life: all these developments had made violent revolution of the communist type impossible. But, because the legend of being a savior of Italy from communism was useful, the frank statement in "Popolo d'Italia" was forgotten and so much propaganda has been circulated about Mussolini's achievements in staving off an imaginary imminent Red revolution that the dictator may now have come to believe this himself, just as Stalin may have been convinced by his own propaganda machine that he, rather than Trotzky, was the main figure responsible for building up the Red Army and winning the Russian civil war.

In Germany also the evidence that Hitler's Third Reich was the sole alternative to communism is not convincing. There was an upsurge of communism in Germany in the years immediately after the war. It was a natural reaction of the more radical workers to the bitter disillusionment over the loss of the war and the hardships of the peace. But the backbone of German Bolshevism was broken in the many little, almost forgotten skirmishes and campaigns and outbursts of street fighting all over Germany in 1918, 1919, and 1920, in years when Hitler played no significant rôle whatever in German political life. The last weak flare-up of militant Communism was in the Hamburg uprising in 1923. After that time, although the Communists polled a substantial vote as a parliamentary party, they at no time resorted to armed rebellion. They represented no threat to public order which the police, without even invoking the aid of the Reichswehr, could not have easily handled. Hitler, in "conquering communism" in 1933, was triumphing over an empty shell, a bogy. In the worst years of the depression the Communists, enjoying full freedom of speech, press, and agitation, never won the support of a majority of the working class, to say nothing of other, more conservative classes in the population. While it is impossible to say with dogmatic certainty what would have been the course of German political events if Hitler had not established his dictatorship, there seems to be no reason to doubt that the republican system could have carried on, with the Communists representing a disgruntled but impotent section of left-wing labor sentiment.

The challenge of collectivism to democracy in politics and individualism in economics is sometimes identified with the challenge of social security. An antithesis is seen as between the ideal of liberty and the ideal of security. Now it is quite true, as the world crisis has shown with painful vividness, that the provision of social security is one of the unsolved problems of democracy. At the same time it is quite mistaken to imagine that the surrender of liberty implied in the organization of the collectivist state is compensated by a gain in security.

It is true that all the dictatorships have been lavish with promises of social security. The new Soviet Constitution assures Soviet citizens "the right to work, the right to rest, and the right of material security in old age, as well as in the event of sickness or the loss of ability to work." Hitler places in the forefront of his achievements the return to work of five million unemployed. Clause 27 of the Italian Fascist Labor Charter promises: [6]

the perfectioning of accident insurance; the improvement and extension of maternity assistance; insurance against the industrial diseases and tuberculosis as a step towards insurance against all forms of sickness; the perfectioning of insurance against involuntary unemployment; the adoption of special forms of endowment insurance for young workers.

The Soviet Union has made the most far-reaching claims in the matter of abolishing economic insecurity; its actual accomplishments in this field, therefore, deserve closer investigation than they have sometimes received. It is significant, for instance, that the Constitution which generously grants everyone the right to work contains no guaranties for the Soviet citizen against forced labor and no assurances that a living wage will be paid. Mere ability to put everyone to work is not necessarily indicative of a system's ability to provide high standards of welfare for the people who live under it. The late dictator Gomez, of Venezuela, found plenty of work for his subjects to do. So does the warden of Sing Sing Prison.

If by abolition of unemployment one means that everyone has work at regular wages and of his own choice, that most desirable ideal has certainly not been realized in Russia. Millions of people, "liqui-

[6] *Cf.* Ion S. Munro, "Through Fascism to World Power" (London: Alexander Maclehose & Co., 1933), p. 349.

dated" kulaks, banished priests, political suspects of all kinds, together with ordinary criminals, have been sent to forced-labor concentration camps during recent years in the Soviet Union. Some light on conditions in these camps is cast by a recent Moscow communiqué which, after announcing the completion of a piece of railway construction in eastern Siberia, entirely with forced labor, casually mentioned that the workers had often been required to stand up to the waist in freezing water. Similar or worse conditions prevailed during the building of the Baltic to White Sea Canal, rushed to completion, with a complete disregard of elementary safety measures for the prisoners employed on it, by the Gay-Pay-Oo. If anyone were given the unpleasant alternative of being on the dole in England or on relief in America or of being shipped off to forced labor on the Moscow-Volga canal or in the Karaganda coal mines or in the timber camps of North Russia, and if all the hardships of both conditions were fairly stated, I do not think there is the slightest doubt that unemployment would seem vastly the lesser evil.

"The right to work," written down in the Soviet Constitution, is a mouth-filling phrase. The obligation to work in a Soviet concentration camp is a much less pleasing reality.

Germany has also achieved its reduction of unemployment in part by labor conscription, although of a milder variety than Russia's. As has already been shown, the amount of real wages paid in Germany has declined by comparison with the depression year 1931; while it is true that more people are employed, it is also true that the living standards of all the employed have declined. Probably few of the unemployed, certainly none of the employed, who vastly outnumber them, in America and Great Britain, would be willing to purchase a reduction or abolition of unemployment at the price of a general worsening of living standards.

The collectivist states erect both figurative and literal barbed-wire barriers to prevent their discontented subjects from escaping. There is no need of similar barriers to keep out a rush of eager immigrants, desirous of sharing their "prosperity" and "security." This test is perhaps more pertinent as regards the Soviet Union, which professes its ability to support a much larger population,[7] than in regard to Germany and Italy, which are already closely settled and overcrowded. As against Russia's approximately million émigrés (this figure would certainly be much larger if it had not been almost impossible during the last decade for Soviet citizens to leave the country, except on some errand or mission approved by the state) there have been perhaps a few thousand immigrants, mostly returned Rus-

---

[7] This is one reason advanced for the recent strenuous propaganda for more births in Russia.

sians who had emigrated to other lands. A former British consul in Leningrad once remarked to me:

In most ports the consul is kept busy looking after sailors who are tempted by the attractions of the place, jump their ships and then find themselves stranded. But I have no cases of that kind here to straighten out. I know of only one British sailor who ever left his ship in Leningrad; and that poor fellow subsequently proved to be crazy.

In short, when it comes to the practical test of living in Russia as a worker, not as a tourist or a member of a fêted delegation, the Soviet Union has no appeal to the unemployed, much less to the employed of America and Western Europe. This is in striking contrast to the experience of the United States, which, before the war, attracted hundreds of thousands of immigrants from Eastern and Southern Europe every year. If the Soviet Union offered, along with unlimited opportunities for work, a standard of living better than that of the unemployed in America and Western Europe the chances are that there would have been a substantial inflow of immigrants into Russia.

While free institutions have not as yet been able to insure social security the lack of these institutions invariably creates a most acute sense of individual insecurity, which cannot be paralleled in democratic countries. No one goes to bed in the latter uncertain whether he may not be waked up in the middle of night, dragged away to a police cell, per-

haps beaten and tortured, probably held for weeks
without knowing of the charge against him, with a
final prospect of being sent to a concentration camp
for an indefinite term without any kind of fair and
open trial. This is just part of the normal routine
of life for the Russian, the German, the Italian.

Another noteworthy consideration in this matter
of security is that, in lands where elections need not
be referred to with quotation marks, the citizens
possess some control over the public purse and hence
over their own private fortunes. Whether this control is always intelligently exercised is another question; but at any rate the possibility of exercising
it is there. The Soviet citizen, on the other hand,
had not the slightest means of self-defense when
his government, by printing excessive amounts of
paper money and by pursuing agricultural and foreign trade policies which inevitably made for a shortage of food and manufactured goods, reduced the
purchasing power of the ruble by 80 or 90 per cent
between 1929 and 1933. The goose-stepping subject of Hitler or Mussolini hasn't the faintest idea
whether his government may not have mortgaged
his last shirt in an effort to keep well to the front
in the wild European armament race.

So, after all, there is good reason for the mixture
of rage and fear which the collectivist dictatorships
display at the faintest signs of surreptitious criticism. If once the mood of hypnotism which they

produced by the combination of mass propaganda
with unlimited terror should collapse, if once the
peoples under their rule could freely discuss and
compare and judge, the whole glittering but jerry-
built edifices, in which hoax and bluff have been such
large ingredients, would be in grave danger of collapse.

There is one field, and only one where the collectivist dictatorship possesses some advantages over
the democracy. This is in militarization and intensive rearmament. A regime subject to the will of
a single irresponsible ruler can arm more swiftly
and secretly than a government which must reckon
with public opinion, unless the latter is convinced
of the reality of the peril with which it is faced.
Moreover the whole routine of life under the modern-style dictatorship, the flood of propaganda, the
rigid regimentation, the frequent parades and demonstrations, the emphasis on the military aspects of
sport and physical training, suggest the armed camp,
the training school for war.

On every other count the collectivist state fails
conspicuously to provide the common man with a
more abundant life. Not only is the level of the
dictatorships incomparably lower than that of the
democracies as regards real wages and salaries and
the cultural and material satisfactions which are
afforded to their subjects; but the collectivist states
have, in many respects, fallen below the standards

of the regimes which preceded them. Not a single problem, raised by the crisis and unsolved in individualist and democratic countries, has been genuinely and satisfactorily solved under collectivism. The causes of complaint have not been removed; all that has happened is that the peoples under the dictatorships have been very vigorously and effectively deprived of the power of voicing complaint.

That democracy has a comfortable, even an overwhelming, margin of advantage over dictatorship by every standard of material well-being, cultural breadth, and educational progress that can be applied, is no final assurance that it will come out the victor in the fierce struggle of rival systems which is such a distinctive characteristic of the present century. History is strewn with the wrecks of higher forms of civilization which, when they had become soft and decadent, were smashed by lower forms, endowed with a stronger measure of fanaticism and brute force—qualities which are not lacking in present-day dictatorships. How does it stand with democracy's chances of survival?

Chapter IV

CAN DEMOCRACY SURVIVE?

BEFORE the war the gradual extension and strengthening of democratic institutions throughout the civilized world seemed to be a reasonable probability. The traditional alternative to democracy, conservative autocracy, was visibly declining in power and prestige. The post-war alternatives to democracy, communism and fascism, had not appeared on the horizon.

Now democracy is definitely on the defensive. There is little prospect of its spread in the face of the cast-iron dictatorships which have been set up in so many countries. What is rather at stake is its survival in those countries where it has struck deepest root, in the United States, Great Britain, with its self-governing Dominions, France, Switzerland, Belgium, the Netherlands, and the Scandinavian countries.

One disconcerting reflection that must have occurred to many observers who, while convinced of the superiority of democracy as a theoretically desirable form of government, are doubtful as to its chances of survival in the present age is that there may be a Gresham's Law in politics, as in economics. Gresham's Law in economics teaches that bad money will always drive good money out of circulation, if the two are given equal currency. In the same way it is conceivable that arbitrary dictatorship may, in the long run, inevitably displace democratic self-government. For the competition between these two systems is, in one respect, very uneven. Democracy may outvote communism and fascism at the polls twenty times, and champions of these alternative systems will rise again to contest the twenty-first election. But let democracy lose one election, held under circumstances of abnormal strain and crisis, to the forces of dictatorship, and it will have no chance to present its case for free consideration at the next one, because every prerequisite of a free election automatically disappears as soon as a communist or fascist regime comes into power.

A democratic system ceases to deserve that name if it does not permit the freest possible peaceful agitation for social and economic change, of the most far-reaching character. By its very nature it cannot employ against communists and fascists their own methods of total and ruthless suppression of all political opponents.

The result is that a dilemma arises which might have perplexed even the lucid liberal intelligence of Voltaire. One of liberty's classical definitions is Voltaire's alleged famous saying: "I disagree utterly with what you say and will defend to the death your right to say it." In the case of ordinary differences of opinion this formula should be axiomatic for any liberal. But one wonders whether even Voltaire would have pronounced it with full heartiness if he had known that his opponent, once in power, would put him in a concentration camp, burn his books, and do everything possible not only to eradicate Voltaire's ideas but to make any free discussion of ideas impossible.

Another point in which democracy, on a surface view, seems at a disadvantage by comparison with dictatorship is in the matter of public criticism, calculated to undermine the regime from within. Imagine what would be the fate of any German or Italian priest who, with however good documentary evidence, should follow in the footsteps of Father Coughlin and publicly give the lie direct to Hitler or Mussolini. Heywood Broun, president of the American Newspaper Guild, has repeatedly expressed in print the opinion that President Roosevelt is "Labor's Public Enemy Number One." One doesn't envisage the head of the Soviet journalists' union, theoretically protected as he is by the far-reaching paper guaranties of the new Soviet Constitution, applying even a much milder critical term to Stalin or, for that matter, to any of Stalin's second or third lieutenants.

But, if democracy is to survive, it must honestly live up to the implications and accept the risks of its basic theory, that the people is sovereign and is entitled to make its choice among the alternative philosophies and the practical measures which may be submitted for its consideration, without any check from self-appointed official guardians. Something of the essential quality of democracy is lost if the smallest and most unpopular minority group is denied the opportunity to state its case, even if that case includes abolition of democratic methods of government and civil liberties. It is a grotesque contradiction in terms to deny freedom of expression in the supposed interests of liberty. Moreover, experience shows that, after a process of suppression has set in, it is very difficult to know where it may stop.

Advocates of democracy will be well advised to leave to the theoreticians of communism and of fascism the manufacture of ingenious rationalizations of the proposition that "true liberty" is best assured by literally or figuratively knocking on the head anyone who expresses disagreement with the dominant philosophy. That democracy may conceivably be overthrown by democratic or semi-democratic means, that communism or fascism, in a time of great national crisis and despair, might win the support of a majority or at least of a sufficiently large and active minority to seize state power and substitute dictatorship for representative government, is simply an additional, perhaps a useful challenge to the democratic method to prove its creative worth.

Nervous individuals who believe that revolutions are the handiwork of individual agitators and mysterious secret societies, rather than the result of fundamental social maladjustments, and who see the salvation of the existing social order in the passing of bigger and better restrictive measures in the form of criminal syndicalism laws and exaction of special oaths of allegiance from teachers, would be well advised to consider the implications of the contrasted experiences of pre-war Russia and pre-war England.

Tsarist Russia was repressed, policed, spied on, protected by every conceivable administrative measure against the public expression of radical or revolutionary ideas. In England any extremist, whether he was advocating a new religion or a new social order, could speak his mind to all who chose to listen in Hyde Park. Socialism before the war, communism and fascism since the war have had every opportunity to convince the British masses. Russia was hermetically sealed against "dangerous thoughts," England fully and voluntarily exposed to them.

If revolutions could be made by "agitators" and stopped by spies and police England, not Russia, should have had the edifice of its social and economic order overthrown by the impact of the World War and the disturbing problems that developed as its sequel. Actually, the Tsarist machine of repression, powerful and imposing as it looked, broke down completely in the crisis of the war. Tsarism fell not because of any cunning conspiracy of revolutionary leaders (every prominent socialist leader was either in prison or in exile when the March Revolution occurred), but because not one regiment of loyal troops could be found to combat the leaderless, spontaneous rebellion of the Petrograd masses. And, after Tsarism had fallen, the very rigor of its former regime of repression, which had paralyzed the Russian faculty for self-government, brought its own historical retribution in the shape of the most tremendous social and economic upheaval of modern times.

Meanwhile England, under all the stresses and strains of the war and post-war periods, with its Communists and Fascists free to talk as they pleased, with its numerous prophets of pessimism filling newspapers and magazines with articles about present and impending symptoms of national doom and decline, has remained pretty much the same England, with a higher standard of living for its population than any European country, its jails free from political prisoners and its government carried on without benefit of firing-squad and concentration camp—those favored methods of communist and fascist dictators in reinforcing the supposedly unanimous enthusiastic loyalty of their subjects. The net result of two decades of unrestrained Communist propaganda has

been the occasional election of a single Communist
to Parliament and the habitual forfeiture by the
Communist Party of the deposit which, under British law, must be paid by the candidate who fails to
poll one-eighth of the votes in a parliamentary contest. A comparison of England and Russia affords a
convincing answer to the question which method affords better insurance against violent social revolution: the method of freedom or the method of
tyranny.

Genuine democracy emphatically means scrupu-
lous maintenance of freedom of speech, press, assembly, and organization for all groups of its citizens. It emphatically does not or should not mean
that armed minority groups should be permitted to
ride roughshod over the rights of the majority.
Every one of the anti-democratic revolutions of the
post-war period could have been averted if the governments which preceded the coming into power of
the communist and fascist regimes had been strong
enough and firm enough to insist that a non-party
army and police should be the sole organs entitled
to use armed force and to suppress the private armies
of Red Guards in Russia, Blackshirts in Italy, Brown-
shirts in Germany which constituted the spearhead
of the revolutionary thrusts for power.

Such repressive measures as the prohibition of private armies, of any political complexion, and the
maintenance of the nonpolitical character of the

army and the police, while necessary and desirable, represent the negative and less important side of democracy's technique of self-preservation. By the time a revolutionary mass movement acquires the momentum of Bolshevism in Russia in 1917 or of Fascism in Italy in 1922 or of National Socialism in Germany in 1933, laws and governmental regulations are swept away like frail dykes before a tidal wave. Whether democracy will survive during the present century depends much more on the answers which future history will give to the following questions:

Can democracy prove sufficiently dynamic, sufficiently active in promoting necessary social and economic changes and adjustments, to retain the unshaken confidence of the majority of the people who still live under free institutions? Will the democratic countries, not one of which, it may significantly be noted, can reasonably be accused of seeking war, be strong enough and sensible enough to remain outside the sphere of such future conflicts as the nationalist ambitions of some states and the clashing trends of communist and fascist fanaticism portend for the future?

"Liberty," Matthew Arnold once said, "is a good horse, but a horse to ride somewhere."

Faced by two aggressively propagandist alternative conceptions of government, democracy with its concomitant, individual liberty, cannot survive as a museum piece, a fetish, a theoretically desirable abstract ideal. It must vindicate itself as a superior means of insuring to the widest possible number of people the better material standard of living, the wider educational and cultural facilities and greater leisure that should be the natural fruits of scientific progress and invention.

True, the record of the democratic states in this respect, as was shown in the last chapter, is incomparably better than that of the collectivist dictatorships. But this is no excuse for complacency and self-satisfaction. It is no very solid and lasting consolation to an American or British worker or employee, out of work through no fault of his own, to be told that many people in Russia and in Germany are doing hard work for less food and compensation than he receives in the form of relief. The proper measure of democracy's achievement is not the conspicuous failure of the dictatorships to provide decent living standards for their peoples, but the creative possibilities of the democratic method itself, which are very far from being fully realized.

There are two points especially in which democracy fails to measure up fully to its own ideals. One is in not living up to its own code of equality of opportunity for all citizens, irrespective of race and religion, class and color, of freedom for expression of dissenting opinion, and of trade-union organization. The other is not clearly grasping the implica-

tions of the machine age and grappling more reso-
lutely and vigorously with the problem of security
which has been presented so vividly and poignantly
by the world crisis, with its mass unemployment.

The victories of America's superb Negro athlete,
Jesse Owens, at the last Olympic Games afford excellent material for reflection both on the superiority
of democracy to dictatorship, which is invariably associated with some acute form of race, class, or nationalist prejudice, and on the failure of democracy,
in America, to fulfill its highest possibilities. If
Owens had been a German subject he could not have
taken part in the competition. The race fanaticism
in Germany has reached a point where the true Nazi
would rather lose an athletic contest than win with
the aid of "non-Aryans." That Owens could compete
on an American team and play such a large part in
rolling up a high score of points is so much to the
credit and advantage of a democratic system. But
how much more the Negro race might have contributed to America if, after emancipation from literal
slavery, it had not been obliged to struggle against
so many forms of social, educational, and occupa-
tional discrimination!

The relative superiority of democracy to another
form of dictatorship, based not on race, but on class
discrimination, found a practical illustration at the
recent Harvard Tercentenary celebration. One of the
eminent scholars who received a degree on this occa-

sion was Professor Michael Rostovtzeff, che distinguished Russian historian of the economic and social aspects of the breakdown of the Roman Empire. Professor Rostovtzeff received his degree not as the representative of Moscow or Leningrad University, but as a Sterling Professor at Yale. He is one of a very large number of notable pre-war Russian scholars who have found in foreign lands the freedom in teaching and research that has been denied to them in their own country ever since unquestioning adherence to Marxian dogma has been required of every scholar in the social sciences.

It is not an accident that no historical work comparable in significance with Professor Rostovtzeff's has been published in Russia since the Revolution. If he had remained in his native country after the Revolution he would, if one may judge from the precedents of the fates of other historians, have been obliged, in the best case, either to teach his chosen subject in a narrow spirit of party dogmatism or to abandon his profession and to seek security in some kind of inconspicuous clerical work. It is by no means impossible that he would have shared the fate of his distinguished colleagues in the historical field, Professors Platonov, Tarle, Lubavsky, and Likhachev all members of the Russian Academy of Sciences, who, with scores of historians and students of lesser note, were arrested by the all-powerful Gay-Pay-Oo, held in close confinement, and cross-examined on some weird trumped-up charges of treason and sabotage until some of the historians, elderly men in indifferent health, sustained complete nervous breakdowns, while Platonov, perhaps the best known Russian historian since Kluchevsky, died in exile.

Universities in all the free countries have derived both honor and practical advantage by providing academic refuges for Russia's fugitive scholars. The Soviet Union's loss is their gain. In precisely the same way the cultural life of Germany has been impoverished and that of other lands has been enriched by the wholesale expulsion of Jews from chairs at the German universities.

Citizens of democratic countries may take justifiable pride in the fact that the flight of scholars is a distinctly one-way movement, from the dictatorships to the democracies. One does not hear of professors leaving Harvard, Oxford, and the Sorbonne to seek undisturbed facilities for creative research in Moscow, Rome, and Berlin.

At the same time culture has not kept pace with the progress of mechanical science. In America especially depth in higher education has been unreasonably sacrificed to breadth, quality to quantity. People now have a far wider range of reading material than their grandfathers or even their fathers; but they read vastly more trash. Radio, the talking picture, and the considerable expansion in foreign cable news services have made possible a much more intimate view of foreign countries; but the view is often distorted by sensationalism and blurred by ignorance.

The vogue enjoyed by political and economic amateurs like Father Coughlin and Dr. Townsend, to say nothing of the Negro "god," Father Divine, would seem to indicate that for considerable classes of the American people education has failed on the lower as well as on the higher levels. A serious international cultural malaise is indicated by the spread of the self-styled "Oxford Group Movement," sponsored by the Rev. Frank N. D. Buchman, with the amazing combination of platitudes and puerilities which it offers for the solution of personal and social problems.

A field in which democracy is still imperfectly realized in the United States is that of labor organization. A strong trade-union movement must be regarded as an integral part of democracy in the industrial age. There is no semblance of economic equality between the large modern industrial corporation, backed by hundreds of millions or billions of dollars of capital, and the individual worker or employee. Employer paternalism in individual cases may be benevolent, but more often is not. While there is a strong case for such measures of social legislation as prohibition of child labor and the establishment of minimum wage scales for women workers, any sweeping attempt to fix wage scales by governmental decree, under an individualist, competitive system, where labor and capital are both free to strike the best possible bargain, seems foredoomed to failure.

So the best, probably the sole guaranty of a wage scale approximately proportioned to the industry's capacity to pay, in the large modern industry, is the existence of a strong, independent trade-union, organized on a national scale, with officials who are freely elected by the workers and who are not dependent on the company concerned for employment. The company or plant union is open to much the same objection that applies to the forms of labor organization which exist under the dictatorial regimes. Like the Soviet trade-union, or the Italian labor syndicate, or the German *Arbeitsfront,* the company union, under favorable conditions, may perform valuable secondary functions in organizing welfare work, excursions, sport, and entertainment. But the worker's primary interest is not in such organized leisure activities, desirable though they are, but rather in his pay and what he can buy with it, and also in the protection which he enjoys against unreasonable speeding-up and unhealthy working conditions. This is where any kind of controlled, paternalistic organization, whether it be a Soviet trade-union, obliged to take orders not from its working-class rank-and-file membership, but from the ruling Communist Party, or a Fascist or Nazi labor organization, which is in precisely the same position, or a company union, with its officials dependent on the employer for employment and promotion, is almost certain to break down.

Any comparison of the economic position of organized and unorganized workers, in America or in any other country, shows, in the overwhelming majority of cases, that wages are higher and working conditions better where independent organization of labor has been firmly established. No reasonable person would suggest that under democracy workers should be coerced into joining a trade-union or any other organization against their will. But in America the coercion which exists is usually in the other direction. There have been repeated refusals of large corporations to deal with trade-unions to which the majority of their employees desired to belong. Some companies have an unenviable record of maintaining staffs of armed guards and labor spies in their plants in order to discover and block any attempt at trade-union organization. This kind of thing savors of dictatorship, not of democracy.

Even from the standpoint of the selfish interest of the employer, the attempt to block and stamp out trade-union organization is extremely shortsighted. For trade-unionism, wherever it has acquired a firm legal footing, has proved itself a moderate and stabilizing, not an extremist and subversive, force. The British trade-unions are a much stronger and more reliable bulwark against communism than the British Fascists. It is not in countries where trade-unionism is strong that one may reasonably look for violent socially revolutionary tendencies among the workers, but rather in lands where the efforts at trade-union organization were always harassed and persecuted, if not suppressed altogether, as in pre-war Russia, Spain, and China.

There are two reasons why trade-unionism operates as a moderate and stabilizing force. In the first place, by improving the material condition of the workers it takes the edge off the appeal of revolutionary agitators, which is naturally in inverse proportion to the well-being of the classes to which it is addressed. Furthermore the process of collective bargaining, with its accompanying insight into business conditions, is an educative process for the labor representatives and is calculated to dispel the illusion that a new heaven and a new earth could be created for labor by the simple process of expropriating all the private owners of industry and turning it over to the state.

In a modern industrial country the right of free trade-union organization ranks with freedom of speech, press, assembly, and election as something that should never be challenged under a democratic system. It may safely be predicted that democracy will become stronger or weaker as this right is generally acknowledged or denied.

The world crisis has naturally produced a spate

of books purporting to offer blueprints for a perfect or at least an improved social and economic order. It is not within the scope of the present work to offer another such blueprint. It is highly probable that there is no universally applicable programme for prosperity. Every country may profitably study the experiences, the successes and failures of its neighbors, but in dealing with the crisis differences of national temperament and historical development, of geography and economics must be considered before it is assumed that a scheme which has worked well in one land would work equally well everywhere else. Quite apart from differences in the political and economic systems, the Soviet Union, with its vast expanse of territory, its undeveloped and partially developed stores of natural wealth, its imperfect network of communications, obviously faces both different possibilities and different problems from those of smaller, thickly settled countries, relatively poor in natural resources, such as Italy and Japan. In the same way a measure that might prove suitable for small, compact, centralized Great Britain might be a failure in the United States, with its immensely greater area, its federal system of government, and its strongly marked economic regional characteristics.

There are, however, two broad objectives which every democratic system should set for itself. The need for attaining these objectives has been made vastly more urgent by the suffering which the crisis brought with it. Democracy's chances of survival are in no small degree bound up with the vigor and momentum and success of its movement toward the realization of these two aims. The first is greater material security for the individual. The second is greater equality of opportunity.

A hundred years, even fifty years ago the impact of an industrial, commercial, and financial depression was less devastating because a much larger part of the people, in American and European countries, lived on the land and was, therefore, self-dependent as regards food and shelter. Moreover, at that time farming was much more self-sufficient and less commercialized; clothing and other manufactured articles were often made on the farm.

Today this form of security has greatly diminished; and there is no prospect of its return. Urbanization of life is a world-wide trend. The advance of mechanization has made it possible to raise much more food with many fewer workers in agriculture. A substantial farm-owning class is an important asset to democracy; and governmental efforts to check the drift toward tenancy and to make farming self-sustaining, even at some cost to the national treasury, are thoroughly justified.

But statistics from all corners of the world indicate that more and more people are dependent for their livelihood on industry, commerce, transportation, and the numerous related occupations and services. In other words, instead of raising most of their own food, manufacturing some of their own homespun clothing and homemade boots, living in their farmhouses, they are paid money wages and are obliged to pay in cash for rent, food, clothing, and other living expenses.

Only utopians dream of reversing the trend of the machine age. The cotton mills of Bombay and Osaka are certain to clothe more Indians than Gandhi's village spinning wheels. Instead of wasting time in lamenting a development that is as inevitable and irresistible as the march of science and invention, intelligent public opinion in democratic countries should endeavor to work out a new programme of security, calculated to meet the needs of a predominantly urban community.

Among the essential items in such a programme are unemployment insurance, compensation for industrial disability and injury, health insurance, and old-age pensions. The details of such a programme, the division of supervision between central and local authorities, the distribution of the burden as between the government, labor, and capital are proper subjects of discussion. But the necessity of enacting a thoroughly adequate programme of social security in the modern industrial state seems beyond any reasonable dispute. It represents the sole practicable means of giving the salary and wage earners of today the security that belonged to the far more numerous self-sufficient farmers and small craftsmen of a century ago.

Besides averting a tremendous amount of human suffering, with its natural and inevitable accompaniment of bitterness against the entire existing social order and readiness to run after every counsel of despair and every quack economic panacea, a well planned and administered system of social security, with its timely payment of increased benefits in periods of stress and depression, would certainly help to mitigate the severity of economic crises. Side by side with comprehensive social security legislation should go a carefully thought out and flexible public works programme, capable of being reduced to a minimum in the fat years of prosperity and of being expanded to the maximum in the lean years of crisis.

It is safe to say that, if America in 1929 had been equipped with a nation-wide system of unemployment insurance and old-age pensions and with a definite plan of national and local public works, the crisis would have been greatly reduced in scope and duration and would have proved much less costly to the taxpayer. In the field of public works, of course, every country is subject to its own geographical and economic limitations. Small, highly industrialized Great Britain, for instance, has not found this method of "made" public work practicable to any great extent in dealing with unemployment. On the other hand the much abused British "dole" has proved to be one of the most humane and practical methods of relieving unemployment distress devised in any country and has been a tremendous force for social stabilization. It furnishes one of the most obvious reasons why the riots and bitter discontent and unrest which characterized the epoch after the end of the Napoleonic wars in England have not been duplicated during the last two decades. Incidentally, the contrast between the stark poverty and misery of the masses in Great Britain in the twenties and thirties of the last century and the minimum well-being which social insurance legislation guarantees to the most unfortunate unemployed today is an admirable object lesson both in the creative possibility of free institutions, so consistently ridiculed and denied by communist and fascist doctrinaires, and in the different social results of rule by an oligarchy and government by a democracy.

In the United States, so different from Great Britain in its expanse of territory and in the variety of its natural resources, there should be less difficulty in employing the method of organized public works along with the method of unemployment insurance as a weapon against unemployment. Flood and drought alike are driving home the necessity of conserving stores of natural wealth that were all too recklessly wasted during the first flush of pioneer exploitation.

Throughout the recent crisis conservatives in America have concentrated their fire on alleged wastefulness in relief methods, while radicals and liberals have stressed the amount of misery that occurred for lack of adequate relief measures. And all too often both types of criticism were justified. To assume on this basis, however, that either widespread wastefulness or widespread suffering in time of depression is an inevitable by-product of the democratic system in politics or of the individualist system in economics, is to fall into unreasonable fatalism. The remedies are at hand: an integrated system of social security measures combined with an orderly scheme of public works could immensely diminish both the neglected suffering and the sporadic waste and extravagance of a future crisis, while simultaneously making a solid long-term investment in future national wealth and welfare.

Social security has naturally been pushed into the foreground by the recent crisis. Equally important, from the standpoint of the successful functioning of a democratic system, is the greatest possible equality of opportunity. Absolute equality of opportunity is as impossible as absolute equality of human personality, because children are inevitably conditioned by the material and cultural environments of their homes, to say nothing of the physical and mental influences of heredity. The Soviet Union, the country where the greatest destruction has been inflicted in the name of equality, of annihilation of class differences, has long abandoned the original dream of some Communists of bringing up all children in state institutions, under conditions of complete equality. And the children of high Soviet officials or industrial managers have an incomparably better chance in life than children who are born to exiled kulak parents in some dreary timber camp, or even to unskilled laborers in the drab and dirty barracks which still represent a large part of Russia's working-class housing.

But while the democratic state cannot level the positions of all families, so that children may start in the race of life from scratch, it can and should, if only as a means of insuring its own stability and orderly development, make every effort to see that no child of marked ability in any field lacks the opportunity for suitable training and education because of poverty. This ideal could be realized through a wider institution of scholarships at state universities and technical and other special schools.

Democracy's prospect of survival in the face of the challenge of communism and of fascism is bound to be in precise proportion to its ability to keep the avenues of advancement, political and economic, unblocked by monopolistic privilege, whether based on birth or on wealth. When a boy who started as a penniless farm laborer in England can become Lord Snell, chairman of the London County Council and holder of many other posts of distinction and public service, his fellow members of the Peerage who trace their pedigrees back to the Norman Conquest can reasonably feel confident that they are a long way from the guillotine.

Envy is as inescapable a condition of human life as the inequality which provokes it. It becomes a formidable form of social nitroglycerine under two conditions: when the masses are conscious of a worsening in their condition, and when a considerable number of individuals endowed with genuine force and ability feel themselves excluded from normal opportunities of advancement, from a fair chance of enjoying a satisfactory livelihood. No revolution can succeed without a large measure of mass support. But the masses who form the parades and fight on the barricades do only the spadework of revolution. Its higher strategy depends on the nucleus of intellectuals and semi-intellectuals who can be identified as making up the leadership of all the three big post-war revolutions.

Al Smith, as the symbolic figure of the poor boy who rises to political and economic leadership and gradually acquires a rather conservative cast of economic thought, is the typical product of a democracy like that of America, where the door of opportunity is still kept fairly wide open. A boy born in Al Smith's circumstances in pre-war Moscow or in Barcelona, endowed with Al Smith's ability, but seeing no escape from a life of poverty and class discrimination under an oppressive and reactionary government and social order, might easily have become an active Bolshevik organizer and, ultimately, a Soviet official in Russia or might be fighting on the Red side of the front as an Anarchist, Socialist, or Communist in Spain.

Examples could be multiplied from historical experience ever since Rome's "Reds" and "Whites" fought and slaughtered each other by turns in the days of Marius and Sulla to show that the greatest threat to democracy, republicanism, and self-governing institutions lies in the topheavy concentration of wealth, power, and privilege in the hands of the few. Social strife and civil war were the natural outcome of the steady accentuation of the opposed extremes of wealth and poverty in the Roman Republic. The emergence of Caesar's absolutism was not a sudden *coup d'état* against a healthy political organism, but the inevitable result of the prolonged decay of the Roman middle-class farm proprietors who had constituted the firmest basis of the republic.

The danger of the decay of democratic institutions from within as a result of excessive concentration of wealth and power in a few hands is also present under modern capitalism. But, so long as the method of liberty is preserved, there are antidotes to this tendency. Strong concentrations of capital can be balanced by strong organizations of labor. If the proverbially grasping middleman becomes too grasping he can be curbed through the competition of efficiently managed coöperatives. So long as there is freedom of the written and spoken word and of the ballot, it is possible to counteract topheavy concentrations of wealth by imposing heavy income and inheritance taxes on large fortunes and to redistribute a considerable part of the accumulations of private wealth for the benefit of social services.

Liberty and democracy are no automatic panaceas. They depend in the last analysis on the public spirit, intelligence, and common sense of the peoples who try to make them work. The most advanced beneficent paper constitution quickly turns into a farce if it is thrust suddenly on a predominantly ignorant, illiterate people with a governmental tradition of arbitrariness and corruption. But other systems also depend on the individual ability and capacity of the people who live under them. The Soviet Union, where for many years it was a matter of Communist dogma to deprecate the importance of the individual personality, has recently made a sharp swing in a different direction, under the compulsion of the needs of its programme of economic development. The speeches of Stalin, Molotov, Ordzhonikidze, and other Soviet leaders during the last years have been filled with references to the vital importance of selecting the right men for the right posts.

In the theory and practice of liberty, democracy possesses an inestimably valuable weapon for achieving necessary social change peacefully. Englishmen have not fought a battle against Englishmen on British soil for two and a half centuries. But this magnificent achievement in social peace, with all that it means in freedom from the arbitrary killings and imprisonments, the constant repression and espionage, the festering embitterment that are certain to be both the accompaniment and the sequel of civil strife, has not been purchased at the price of stagnant acquiescence in the *status quo*. England's achievements in full democratization of political life and in advanced social legislation compare favorably with those of several countries which have found it necessary to resort to the costly process of violent revolution and civil war.

So there is no cause of decline and decay inherent in the nature of democracy. Liberty is a constant agency of self-renovation. Now, as always, democratic regimes are faced with some dangers. There is danger, in times of great stress and crisis, from the agitation of the advocates of communism and fascism. There is more real danger in the existence of the hidebound reactionary type of mind, which, by opposing the mildest and most necessary measures of change and reform, plays admirably into the hands of the apostle of violent revolution. But in countries with a long democratic tradition both the reactionary and the apostle of violent upheaval tend to fade into relative insignificance.

In Great Britain the Communists have occasionally been able to elect one member of Parliament; the Fascists have not achieved even this modest measure of success at the polls. If one may judge from the election returns almost twenty years of propaganda have not converted a quarter of one per cent of America's voters to a belief in the doctrines of communism. At this rate of progress it would be several centuries before communism could be regarded as a serious minority force in American politics.

There is much talk in American radical and liberal circles of the supposed danger of fascism. And it is certainly most probable that, if American democracy should ever be overthrown, it would yield place to fascism, not to communism. Both communism and fascism are forms of despair politics. But communism is calculated to appeal to people who never had anything, while fascism is the preferred expression of despair for people who once had something, but have lost it.

But when one tries to find precisely where the alleged fascist menace to America lies, the clues are few and unconvincing. There is no personality, no movement in America today that even remotely suggests the beginnings of Italian Fascism or German National Socialism. American Communists, determined to invent fascism if it did not exist, made a ludicrously clumsy and ineffectual effort to depict Governor Landon, a typical product of one of the most socially democratic states in America, as a budding *Duce* or *Führer*. There could be no better commentary on this effort than the following excerpts from Governor Landon's address before the Kansas state convention of the American Legion:

First is the duty of tolerance. It ought not be necessary to stress tolerance in America. We have a great tradition of tolerance growing out of the fundamentals of the past. . . . Also, we must insist upon the preservation and protection of American freedom, and, above all, the freedom of expression. So long as we have freedom of expression and a free exchange of ideas many of our most serious problems will solve themselves. Thirdly and finally, I emphasize our duty in preserving peace. Those of us who were in the service appreciate in a way others cannot the utter futility of war. I need not tell you of its waste, its meaningless cruelty. You know.

Tolerance, freedom of expression, and "the utter futility of war" are not the themes which one associates with the oratory of Hitler and Mussolini.

Much confusion of thought has been caused in America because unintelligent conservatives have developed the habit of calling almost anyone with whom they disagree a "communist"; the idea that President Roosevelt is a communist, for instance, is quite as absurd as the suggestion that Governor Landon is a fascist. Unintelligent radicals, in turn, are apt to hiss the epithet "fascist" at anyone who has earned their displeasure, without showing any desire or capacity to discriminate between authentic fascists, conservative upholders of the *status quo* and moderate liberals. When one sifts out the genuine communists and fascists from the controversial clamor, both are found to constitute small and uninfluential fringes of extremist opinion.

So there is little indication that either direct communist or fascist propaganda or internal weaknesses of the democratic system will bring about the overthrow of free institutions in countries where they have become firmly established and represent a definite part of the national tradition. Another factor that must be considered in estimating democracy's chances of survival is the ability of the democratic countries to stand aloof from future wars.

Chapter V

DEMOCRACY AND THE PROBLEM OF PEACE

WAR is the generator of revolutions and dictatorships. A nation at war instinctively and inevitably adopts the technique of intensive propaganda, combined with terrorism against war resisters and critics, that is the normal method of peace-time rule under a dictatorship. Even in time of war a democratic tradition is not entirely obliterated. Pacifist and anti-war sentiment had far more chance of expression in America, Great Britain, and France during the war than the critic or dissenter has in the Soviet Union, Germany, and Italy in time of peace. But in the main the war pattern is the pattern of dictatorship.

There are two ways in which a democratic regime is endangered by war. There have been repeated historical examples, of which Napoleon is only the most conspicuous, of the popular and successful military leader subsequently setting himself up as a dictator. Somehow this prospect seems to diminish under the conditions of modern warfare.

It is not accident or sentimentality that has led nations to erect altars to the Unknown Soldier. It is no mere coincidence that neither Foch nor Haig, nor Pershing nor any other leader of the victorious armies of the World War subsequently played any notable rôle in the political life of his country. Modern war is at once so vast and so mechanized that the personalities of its generals, however strong and vivid, tend to become dwarfed. They, like the men under them, are cogs in a huge impersonal machine.

So the likelihood of a democratic system's being overthrown as a result of the ambition and the popularity of a victorious military leader is not so great as it might have been a century ago. Far more probable is the replacement of democracy by some form of dictatorship as a result of crushing military defeat. The time has passed when war was a sort of glorified game of chess, in which rulers could indulge languidly or energetically, as they might choose, in which the stakes were the gain or loss of a province or a colony, the paying and receiving of a monetary indemnity.

The World War has shown that any large-scale conflict between great powers is certain to turn into a bitter-end struggle, with no quarter asked or given, because the penalty for the leadership of the losing side is political, if not physical destruction. Every defeated power in the World War experienced a revolution; most of them, to be sure, experienced secondary revolutions, or counter-revolutions, which partially restored to power the classes which had been ousted in the first shock and bitterness of defeat. Russia, although it was reckoned among the Allies, must also be considered a defeated power, because the issue of its campaigns was almost invariably disastrous. Italy also developed a somewhat defeatist psychology, because its showing in the war was much weaker than that of England and France and it came off very badly in the distribution of the spoils. So, while a democratic regime would probably survive a victory in a military struggle, it would almost certainly succumb to a defeat.

The initiative for the next world conflict, should such a catastrophe befall modern civilization, will certainly not come from any democratically governed state. The most hostile critic cannot reasonably see in the present policies of America, Great Britain, France, and the smaller democracies of Europe any trend toward aggression, anything that remotely suggests the intention of violating the frontiers or seizing the territory of other states.

It would probably be unfair to accuse any government at the present time of deliberately desiring war. It would certainly be irrational for any country, however strongly armed and well provided with natural resources, to assume the tremendous risks of modern war, if it could substantially get its way by other means.

But it is also true that no government in 1914 positively desired an appeal to arms; yet the World War occurred notwithstanding. And the policies and actions that, judged from previous experience, are likely to lead to war—militarization of whole populations, sabre-rattling speeches, direct and indirect interference in the internal affairs of other countries, glorification of war in the abstract, and the use of military phraseology in civil affairs—these are today the distinctive characteristics of the dictatorships, not of the democracies.

Democracy, in conspicuous contrast to communism and fascism, has no sense of a world crusading mission. There is no democratic "international," with headquarters in Washington, London, Paris and dominated by the ruling party of America, Great Britain, or France, sending out agents and propaganda to stir up disaffection in non-democratic countries, as the Communist International, with headquarters in Moscow, tries to overthrow non-Communist governments in all parts of the world. When civil class war flared up in Spain, it was the communist and fascist states that rushed to take sides, while the democratic powers endeavored to maintain a policy of nonintervention.

In contrast to certain dictatorships, democratic countries which lack colonies contrive to get on without them and somehow succeed in maintaining very satisfactory standards of living in the process. Taken by and large, Switzerland and Sweden, Denmark and Norway, which possess no colonies, are as prosperous as the Netherlands and Belgium, with their large colonial empires, and much better off than Portugal, with its large African possessions.

The impulse to territorial and colonial expansion is much stronger in the fascist countries, Germany and Italy, than in the communist Union of Soviet Socialist Republics. Differences of geography and economics are much more important in this connection than differences of political systems. Whatever else may be said in criticism of the Tsarist system, Tsarist imperialism had reaped rich fruits for the Soviet Union to inherit. In the course of its steady march southward and eastward it obtained for the Russian Empire the cotton and cattle lands of Central Asia, the oil and manganese of the Caucasus. Despite Bolshevik lip service to the principle of self-determination of non-Russian nationalities, the Red Army was always at hand to smash any separatist movements in the non-Russian regions which had been annexed before the Revolution.

Consequently the Soviet Union, like the United States and the British Empire, represents a much more balanced, self-contained and naturally rich economic unit than Germany and Italy. Had there been no Bolshevik Revolution, no Soviet system, it is quite probable that Russia would have naturally taken its place with the sated, rather than with the dissatisfied, powers.

These considerations make the present-day foreign policy of Stalin less aggressive than that of Hitler and Mussolini. But if one takes a long-term view of the future, Russia's adherence to its professed ideals of peace seems more questionable. No government in the world has imposed greater sacrifices on its people for the sake of intensive armament than the Soviet regime in Russia. If Germans are sometimes obliged to eat their bread without butter in order to obtain the necessary materials for manufacturing airplanes, cannon, and tanks, Russians have sometimes had to forgo bread altogether.

The officially recorded Soviet expenditure for military and naval purposes increased tenfold, from 1,421,000,000 rubles to 14,815,000,000 rubles, during the three-year period, 1933–1936. During the same years the strength of the Soviet standing army grew from 500,000 to 1,300,000, and there was a far greater increase in the provision of the country with the most modern weapons of warfare, special attention being paid to the air and motorized branches of the service. Militarized physical training transformed a large part of the able-bodied population into promising recruits.

No country in the present disturbed state of the world can afford to dispense with adequate means of self-defense. But the Soviet war preparations, which began much earlier than those of Germany (1929, the year when the first Five Year Plan went into operation, may also be considered the date of the beginning of Russia's intensive armament), and which are based on much greater natural resources than those of the two powers which the Soviet Government considers especially hostile, Germany and Japan, may quite conceivably within another decade go far beyond the needs of defense and give the Soviet Union a position of clear military predominance on the European continent.

There can be no certainty that such a predominance would be used for peaceful ends. The obvious historical analogy, with the French Revolution, is not encouraging. The French Revolution, after the so-called Thermidorian period of relative moderation and reaction from the excesses of the Terror, became involved in the long cycle of the Napoleonic wars. The energy that was generated by the Revolution spent itself on battlefields all over Europe. The Soviet Union now seems to have entered on something like a Thermidorian period, with authority reestablished in factory and schoolroom, with divorces discouraged and a high birth rate demanded, with old titles for military officers restored and a steadily growing inequality between the well-to-do and the poorer classes. Can there be any guaranty that a Russian form of Bonapartism will not some day succeed the Russian Thermidor?

The strong international element in the original

ideals of the Russian Revolution is being deliberately soft-pedalled and shelved in these days, when the moderate turn in the foreign policy of the Soviet Government, represented by adherence to the League of Nations and the conclusion of a military alliance with France, is accompanied by a corresponding moderate turn in the policies of the various Communist parties outside of Russia. This finds expression in more or less successful efforts to form "popular fronts," or coalitions not only with Social Democrats, but also with "bourgeois" liberal and radical groups.

But only the future can show whether Russia's Communist leaders have put away permanently their dream of world revolution. The Red Army soldier still takes an oath to fight for the world revolution. Lenin's works remain the political Bible of Russia's youth; and one finds in Lenin's writings and speeches an abundance of positive dogmatic statements to the effect that the Russian Revolution cannot succeed except as part of an international revolution, and that the Soviet regime cannot endure indefinitely in a capitalist environment. So in 1918 he said:

World-wide imperialism and the triumphal march of a social revolution cannot live side by side. . . . Our backwardness has pushed us forward, and we shall perish if we cannot hold out until we meet a mighty support on the part of the insurrectionary workers of other countries.[1]

[1] Cited by Leon Trotzky, "The History of the Russian Revolution," Vol. III, p. 396.

Still more significant was his declaration in 1920, when the Russian civil war and the Allied intervention had virtually ended:

We have now passed from war to peace. But we have not forgotten that war will come again. So long as both capitalism and socialism remain we cannot live in peace. Either the one or the other in the long run will conquer. There will be a funeral chant either for the Soviet Republic or for world capitalism.[2]

On another occasion Lenin outlined the following programme of action to be followed by a socialist government in power:[3]

The victory of socialism in the beginning is possible in a few capitalist countries or even in one capitalist country. The victorious proletariat of that country, having expropriated the capitalists and organized socialist production in its own country, would rise against the remaining capitalist world, attracting to itself the oppressed classes of other countries, arousing them to uprising against the capitalists, coming out, if necessary, even with armed force against the exploiting classes and their states.

The first part of this programme has been achieved in Russia: the "capitalists," down to the last peasant with twenty acres and two cows, have been expropriated; a big programme of industrial reconstruction, with special emphasis on war industries, has been carried out. Will the Soviet Union, when the time

[2] *Ibid.*, p. 398.
[3] *Cf.* Lenin's "Collected Works" (Russian ed.), Vol. XIII, p. 133.

seems ripe, "rise against the remaining capitalist world," in accordance with Lenin's injunction, using armed force "against the exploiting classes and their states"? It would be premature to give a definite reply to this question. But, if certain passages in Adolf Hitler's "Mein Kampf" may fairly be cited to illustrate the restless expansiveness of Germany's foreign political aspirations under Hitler's leadership equally many militant excerpts in the writings of Lenin can be found to show the explosive possibilities of Bolshevik doctrine. These possibilities may easily manifest themselves as soon as the more pressing difficulties of internal reconstruction, such as the organization of adequate food supply and transportation services, have been overcome and the equipment of the largest standing army in the world with modern implements of destruction has been completed. It is quite conceivable that Soviet campaigns of aggression, either in the East or in the West, could pursue essentially nationalist objectives under a revolutionary phraseology, like the French campaigns to achieve the Rhine frontier after the Revolution.

In the case of the democratic countries there is no reason to suspect the permanence or sincerity of their devotion to the cause of peace. They have no messages from supposedly infallible leaders to the effect that their own survival depends on the overthrow of alternative systems of government. They are perfectly willing to exist side by side with the dictatorships and to let the material and cultural results of the two forms of government speak for themselves.

However, Abyssinia and Manchuria furnish only the most recent of many proofs that to desire peace is not necessarily to obtain it. By what means can democratic countries hope to avoid being involved in future wars? The whole trend of world events during the last years indicates that war cannot be exorcised either through promises not to indulge in it or through any scheme of international organization that is feasible in the present stage of human development.

The Kellogg Pact, with its solemn outlawry of war, has merely placed a premium on the practice of starting war without the formality of a declaration. The League of Nations, weakened from the beginning by the absence of America and further diminished in real authority by the secession of Japan and Germany and the contemptuous flouting of its authority by Italy, has definitely failed to organize effective common action against an aggressor in the two major international crises which were precipitated by the Japanese occupation of Manchuria in 1931 and the invasion of Abyssinia by Italy in 1935.

The League will just as certainly fail in any future similar crisis, and for the same fundamental reason: that no country today is prepared to go to war or even to run serious risk of becoming involved

in war except for the sake of more vital national interests than abstract considerations of right and justice. A number of pleasant illusions have been or
should have been mercilessly shattered by the course
of affairs in Manchuria and Abyssinia. One such
illusion is that wars can be stopped and ambitions
curbed by having an incomplete group of states, calling itself a League of Nations, pass moral resolutions.

Another illusion that must be discarded is that
peaceful means of pressure, such as economic boycott,
can stop a dictator on the warpath. Once a powerful
state has embarked on hostilities it can be stopped only
by warlike measures or by economic measures so
strong that they are likely, if not certain, to lead to
war. This is perhaps the clearest lesson to be drawn
from Mussolini's successful defiance of the League
in the conquest of Abyssinia. Weak sanctions, such
as the curtailment of purchases of Italian goods,
could not seriously affect the course of the war.
Strong sanctions, such as the closing of the Suez
Canal and the stoppage of Italy's oil supplies, were
ruled out because they might have led to war.

Two phrases which seem to bear little relation
to the realities of the present-day world, but which
have exerted an almost hypnotic influence on the
thinking of some earnest friends of peace are "collective security" and "the indivisibility of peace."
The latter, with its implication that any war is destined to turn into a world conflict, has been dis-

proved at least a score of times since the end of the World War. Greece and Turkey fought out their differences on the plains of Asia Minor; Bolivia and Paraguay waged a sanguinary struggle in the jungles of the Chaco; Japan occupied Manchuria; Italy launched her war of aggression in Abyssinia. Had peace been really "indivisible," all these conflicts and many others which have occurred since the end of the World War should have assumed world dimensions. While it is certainly regrettable that war has not been banished entirely from the earth, it would be still more disastrous if every small clash were automatically bound to draw in all countries and to assume the proportions of the World War.

Even a larger war, if past experience is any guide, could easily be localized if the countries which were not directly affected kept their heads. No third power became involved in the Franco-Prussian War of 1870–1871, or in the Russo-Japanese War of 1904–1905. If the Soviet Union should ever become involved in hostilities with Germany or with Japan, or with both these countries, there is absolutely no valid reason why the United States should intervene on either side. There is also a fair prospect that Great Britain might remain isolated from such a conflict, although its position is, of course, made more difficult by its proximity to the European continent and by its extensive interests in the Far East.

Collective security is an unrealizable conception because there is no equality of risk as between the various great powers at the present time. A country that is in no danger, or in very slight danger, of being attacked cannot reasonably be expected to assume responsibility for the defense of the frontier of another country which is much more exposed to attack, especially when the foreign policy of the second country, over which the first country has no control, may be a factor in provoking attack and aggression.

This proposition finds a number of recent concrete illustrations. Clemenceau's suggestion, at the time of the Versailles Conference, that America, along with Great Britain, should permanently guarantee the French eastern frontier never stood the slightest chance of acceptance by American public opinion. It would have meant that America, without any compensating advantage, should assume the onerous and dangerous responsibility of insuring France against any new unfavorable turn in the European balance of power.

The same consideration explains the coolness with which British public opinion reacts to the suggestion of a British guaranty for the Soviet frontier. The Soviet Union can offer no corresponding security to the British Empire. The great majority of Englishmen are agreed that Great Britain must support France against any unprovoked attack, not only as a matter of treaty obligation, but because England's own safety would be most seriously threatened if Germany should crush France and establish itself on the English Channel. But there is a strong and so far invincible unwillingness on the part of the British people to undertake any commitments in Eastern Europe apart from the general obligations of the League Covenant, which, if Abyssinia's experience is an object lesson, are of little practical significance in a crisis.

France, so insistent on the principle of collective security where it works to her national advantage, in Europe, displayed almost complete indifference to it when it was a matter of protecting China and Abyssinia against Japan and Italy. The Soviet Union, eager to exploit the principle of collective security in order to win allies against Germany and Japan, proved unwilling to make the small sacrifice of the receipts of its oil sales to Italy when the idea of collective security was put to a practical test in the case of Abyssinia.

High-sounding phrases like "collective security" and "the indivisibility of peace" are likely to harm rather than help the future prospects of peace. Their application would be apt to extend rather than to contract the area of a future international conflict.

What then should be the peace strategy of the democratic powers? The first regrettable but unavoidable necessity is to be adequately armed for defense. Disarmament and dictatorship simply do not go together. It would be criminal folly for the liberty-loving peoples to be without proper means of self-defense when the regimented thought and the regimented economics of the dictatorships are concentrated so intensively on warlike preparations. Typical of this concentration are the recent displays of cannon at a German "harvest thanksgiving" festival and the vigorous efforts of young Soviet Russians to perfect themselves in parachute jumping in order to be able to participate in the maneuver, on which the Red Army sets great store, of dropping detachments of machine-gunners in the rear of a hostile army.

Fortunately the geographical position and the economic resources of two of the greatest democracies, the United States and Great Britain, with its self-governing Dominions, make it possible to assure national defense without the total militarization of the population that is the ideal and, to a large extent, the practice of the contemporary dictatorships. England is not likely to be attacked directly so long as it maintains a navy second to none and a correspondingly powerful air force. Proximity to the European continent and far-flung imperial interests unquestionably make the British problem of keeping out of war more complicated than the American. But, given the combination of impressive striking power and a determination to avoid rash and sweeping commitments and a skillful and patient diplomacy, it would seem that England's chances of staying out of future wars should reasonably be rated as better than even.

America is of all large nations the best safe-guarded by nature against attack. With no conceivable military rival in her own hemisphere and with two broad oceans for eastern and western frontiers it would seem that America has no possible cause or excuse for going to war so long as it adheres to President Roosevelt's formula of "defending ourselves and defending our neighborhood." The combination of sea and air power, backed by unsurpassed natural and industrial resources and by a location thousands of miles away from any conceivable enemy is calculated to make America absolutely immune from the danger of foreign invasion.

Of the three leading democracies France is in the most difficult position as regards the problem of remaining out of war. Were France content with security behind its underground Chinese wall, in the shape of the huge defensive system that has been constructed along the German border it is very unlikely that it would be subjected to a German attack which would inevitably bring in England as the guarantor of the French frontier. But France is tied up with various pacts, agreements and alliances, of varying degrees of reliability, in Eastern Europe, of which the latest and most significant is the Franco-

Russian alliance. Faced with a militant Germany, superior both in man power and in industrial resources, France understandably seeks allies where it can find them.

But there are grave risks, as well as possibilities of aid in the case of military need, in this Russian alliance. The outbreak of civil war in Spain has shown one of these risks. While the democratic countries stood aloof, leaving the issue to be settled by the balance of forces within Spain itself, the impulse of the dictatorships was to rush to the aid of the side with which they sympathized. The possibilities of this kind of competition in intervention are dangerous enough in Spain. There are other countries—Poland, for instance, or any of the Baltic States—where an outburst of domestic civil war, followed by Russian and German intervention on opposite sides, would almost certainly lead to outright war between Germany and the Soviet Union. France might thus find itself under strong pressure to participate in a war which, on the Russian side, would be a crusade for the achievement of the aims of the Communist International, with which the overwhelming majority of Frenchmen are certainly not in sympathy.

Adequate preparedness for defense does not or should not exhaust the peace strategy of the democratic countries. It goes without saying that there should be complete abstention from any policies of aggression. The foolish idea that contributed so much to draw America into the World War, the idea that a nation's armed forces should be at the disposal of a citizen who takes unwarrantable risks in a war zone, should be definitely scrapped. The economics and the morality of going to war to protect a booming munitions and war supplies trade with one set of belligerent powers should be subjected to a good deal more critical analysis than it received in America in 1917.

There should be a consistent, determined effort to remove the economic causes of war by eliminating the innumerable fetters and strait-jackets on international trade in the form of prohibitive tariffs, quota systems, currencies that are valueless outside the frontiers of a single country. Here, of course, progress cannot be unilateral. If the Soviet Union, Germany, and Italy deliberately shut themselves off from the benefits of freer trade in order to pursue the goal of self-sufficient autarchy, this is their own affair. The democratic countries obviously cannot prevent them from pursuing economic policies which, as past and recent experience indicates, lead to increased poverty and deprivation. Just as obviously the dictatorships have only themselves to blame for the inevitable results of their own policies.

Equality of economic opportunity in all colonies and regions administered under League of Nations mandates is another principle which should be observed in the effort to eliminate the economic causes of war. This brings up the thorny question of possession of colonies and of access to raw materials, the alleged denial of which is often cited as a major grievance of such dissatisfied powers as Germany and Italy. The latter country has now helped itself to a vast colonial empire in East Africa; the future will show whether the profits of an Abyssinia that is now marked out as an Italian economic preserve will pay for the costs of the war and the occupation. It would be difficult to give an affirmative reply to this question on the basis of the evidence at hand.

As for Germany, the return of its former colonies might be a solace from the standpoint of prestige. But the contribution of these colonies to Germany's pre-war economic well-being was negligible; their cost of upkeep, on balance, was far in excess of the trade and investment profits which Germany derived from their possession. There is, therefore, no reason to suppose that the return of these colonies would provide additional employment or raise the German standard of living to any appreciable degree.

So far as access to raw materials is concerned, this has never been denied. Producers during the recent world crisis have been only too eager to find purchasers. The German or Italian importer can buy the products of French and British colonies at the same prices and on the same terms as his British or French competitor.

Countries without colonies or with unimportant and barren colonies do indeed suffer from one important economic disadvantage, compared with powers which possess rich colonial empires. This is in the matter of means of payment. The monetary system of a colonial dependency is naturally linked with that of the power on which it is dependent. If, for example, Germany, instead of Great Britain, ruled India today the mark or some currency based on the mark would be legal tender in India, and Germany's ability to purchase Indian products would be correspondingly enhanced.

But this disadvantage, while it is a genuine one, is extremely difficult to remedy. The restoration of Germany's unimportant pre-war colonies would afford negligible relief. A world currency, equally valid in every country, would provide a theoretical solution for the problem; but this is obviously outside the scope of practical possibilities in the present-day world. Moreover, any such scheme would be especially unacceptable to the collectivist dictatorships, all of which are anxious to retain the fullest power of control and manipulation over their own currency systems.

It is also significant that Switzerland and the Scandinavian countries have never experienced any special difficulties in obtaining such foreign raw materials as they need for their industries, despite the fact that they possess no colonies. There are several causes, some of them peculiar to the conditions of the separate countries, for the food and raw materials shortage which has marked the path of collectivist dictatorship in the Soviet Union, in Germany, and in Italy. But one cause is common to all three countries: a frantic pace of rearmament that throws the mechanism of normal international trade out of gear and makes it necessary to deprive the populations of imported comforts and even necessities in order to keep the wheels of the munitions factories turning faster. A regime like that in Germany, which openly prefers cannon to butter has only its own policy to blame if the simplest peace-time requirements of its citizens, in so far as these depend on the necessarily limited imports from abroad, are starved. It is safe to predict that the complaints about insufficient access to raw materials will lose all their acuteness if and when the present armament race is brought to a stop and a more healthy and natural exchange of goods and services between the various countries can be resumed.

Study of the results and lessons of the World War should help democratic countries to frame their peace policies today. For this last great international conflict showed with convincing vividness both what war can accomplish and what it cannot accomplish.

Despite its horrifying cost in human, cultural, and material values (a cost that is bound to rise in giddy progression as the implements of destruction become more effective), war must still be accepted as a hateful but unavoidable necessity in one, and only in one contingency. This is when it is a country's sole means of resisting invasion and subjugation by an aggressive foreign power.

Victors and vanquished suffered in the economic aftermath of the World War. But it is impossible to deny that France and Great Britain suffered less than Germany and much less than they would have suffered if they had been defeated in the World War. So war can be justified, except from the standpoint of the absolute pacifist and advocate of nonviolence, if it is the sole alternative to submission to a foreign conqueror. It may also be justified if it takes the form of rebellion against foreign oppression or of revolt against an autocracy or a dictatorship that gives no opportunity for the free expression of opposition sentiment.

But war for any other purpose is foredoomed to dismal futility. There is still lively discussion about the motives which impelled America to participate in the World War. The evidence in the case seems to be against the advocates of both extreme viewpoints, those who insist that America went to war as to a holy crusade and those who believe that America's entrance into the conflict was exclusively dictated by bankers and munition makers, actuated by the most sordid considerations of private gain.

Dispassionate analysis shows that idealistic and materialistic motives were almost inextricably blended in America's decision. There is no reason to doubt that President Wilson and many other leaders of American public opinion sincerely saw in the war an instrument for promoting the world-wide triumph of democracy and the establishment of world peace on a permanent and enduring basis. It is also unmistakably true that America had been carrying on an extremely profitable and abnormally swollen trade in munitions and supplies with one group of belligerents, while all commercial contact with the other group was cut off by the Allied blockade. The price of peace, after Germany decided to strike back at the strangling Allied blockade by going over to a counter blockade through the ruthless, unlimited use of the new submarine weapon, would have been the drastic curtailment of this trade. This price America was unwilling to pay.

Now both from the standpoint of promoting democracy and world peace and from the standpoint of advancing national economic interests America's participation in the war, viewed in the retrospect of two decades, must be reckoned a dismal and unmitigated failure. What a mockery the slogan of a world made safe for democracy seems amid the orgy of Europe's triumphant dictatorships!

From the narrower and more selfish standpoint also America's participation was far from successful. Twenty-five billion dollars of additional national debt and ten billion dollars of uncollected and uncollectible war debts represent a rather unreasonable price for the ephemeral boom prosperity which shone for a time on manufacturers, laborers, and farmers as a result of the free-handed governmental spending of war-time economics. If wholesale spending of public funds is a sure cure for depression the money to be spent could be applied to more constructive purposes than war.

As regards the theoretical right of American citizens to travel freely in war zones and to trade with belligerents, everyone with the least sense of realism knows that this right will not be respected for a moment if a new life-and-death struggle on a large international scale breaks out. Any nation situated as Germany was in the World War is bound to hit back with the submarine or with any other weapon that science may devise. One of the soundest and sanest impulses in contemporary American public opinion is the widespread aversion to any action, political or economic, which might involve the country in another war, the general insistence that peace should be valued more highly than war-time profits. One may only hope that this mood will persist in the face of any possible new temptation.

War may perform an emergency negative function: self-defense against unprovoked aggression. It most emphatically cannot realize any positive ideal, such as spreading democracy or establishing uniformly just boundaries or inaugurating a rule of ordered law in international affairs. It cannot do any of these things because the modern totalitarian war, like the modern totalitarian state, inevitably employs as one of its chief weapons unlimited passionate and mendacious propaganda against the enemy. It is beside the point to censure Wilson's doctrinaire cast of mind, or Clemenceau's vindictiveness or Lloyd George's flighty improvisations for what happened at Versailles. A just and reasonable peace could not have been made by any statesmen in the world, acting under the influence of white-hot public opinion at home, inflamed to the last degree by the sufferings and sacrifices of the war and by the hate preachings of the host of regular and volunteer propagandists.

In the same way war can never promote the prosperity of a nation's economy, viewed as a whole. Individuals and groups may make large profits; but for the vast majority of the peoples victory means only a great increase in the burden of debt and taxes, and defeat a wiping out of all savings through inflation, with the additional misery and brutality of class strife and civil war quite probably thrown in for good measure.

So, while the peace strategy of the democratic powers inevitably varies in each case because of dif-

fering geographical and political factors, certain elements in it seem clearly dictated by the lessons of
the World War and the more recent developments
of the post-war period. Adequate preparation for
defense is an essential element in this strategy. While
no chance, however slight, of promoting limitation
or reduction of armaments should be neglected, democratic countries, for the sake of their own free institutions, cannot afford to fall into a position of military inferiority to the dictatorships.

It is the obligation of every government that is
concerned for the maintenance of peace to strike at
the economic causes of war by sponsoring economic
disarmament through mutual abatement of the re-
strictions which have so heavily reduced the volume
of international trade, thereby, in the long run, im-
poverishing every country. Finally, democratic countries which wish to keep out of war will find their
chances of achieving this end greatly enhanced if
they eschew phrases and policies that would tend to
universalize rather than to localize future possible
conflicts and confine themselves, so far as possible, to
the defense of their own boundaries, instead of trying to act as policemen for the whole world.

It is especially to be hoped that the democratic
peoples will remain unimpressed either by Hitler's
trumpet call for a united front against Bolshevism or
by Litvinov's siren plea for "collective security."
War in any part of the world would be a frightful

calamity; and every reasonable diplomatic effort should be made to avert it. But if the hostility of the rival fanaticisms of communism and fascism should be too strong to be restrained, if the Soviet Union and one or more of the fascist countries should ever proceed from exchanges of abuse to a trial of strength in arms the policy of the democratic powers should certainly be one of strict nonintervention. The World War, so far as it was a crusade for democracy, proved to be a complete disillusionment. It would certainly be a tragic irony if any democratic country, after this impressive lesson, should take up arms to make the world safer for either of the post-war forms of tyranny.

Chapter VI

THE CASE AGAINST LIBERTY

INDIVIDUAL liberty and political democracy have always been faced by the opposition of alternative theories of human conduct and political organization. There was a time when absolute monarchs and churches that reached out for temporal power were the main enemies of freedom. Today kings and priests in the main have given way to communist and fascist dictators. But the struggle in the realm of ideas goes on. The post-war reaction against democracy has revived some old arguments against liberty and created some new ones. What, in brief, is the case against liberty?

One accusation against democracy in which there is a curious united front between communists, fascists, and extreme tories who yearn for the supposedly good old days of the Middle Ages is that it favors the growth of plutocracy and grinds the faces of the poor. On this point there is much common ground between the old-fashioned aristocrat who has never accepted the French Revolution and the disciples of Lenin, Hitler, and Mussolini.

174

Closely related to this accusation is the claim that democracy is a sham and fraud, that capitalists and special interests utilize its forms in order to deceive, exploit, and rule the masses of the people. The alleged unreality of what he called "bourgeois democracy" was one of Lenin's favorite arguments for proletarian dictatorship as a transitional stage to the perfect, classless society of communism, where the state itself would "wither away" and disappear. Lenin argued that, even in countries where constitutional guaranties of political and civil liberty were maintained, the capitalists, because of their wealth, could mislead public opinion and influence the course of elections by buying the largest newspapers, engaging the best halls for the meetings of the political parties which they favored, etc.

Consciously or unconsciously Mussolini and Hitler have chimed in with many of Lenin's antidemocratic arguments. Fascist and National Socialist spokesmen declare that the press of their respective countries is the freest in the world, because it serves the whole nation, and not the special interests of small groups of capitalists.

A favorite conservative argument against democracy has been that it would lead to the destruction of public credit and of the rights of property. This thesis is put forward with great force in a well known letter from Lord Macaulay to an American friend. The distinguished Whig historian foresaw a wholesale collapse of public and private obligations at the incitation of the "demagogues" who would arise in times of crisis and take advantage of the opportunities offered by universal suffrage.

It has also been laid to the charge of democracy that it leads to deadening uniformity, to the creation of a mass mind on a level of mediocrity, to the suppression, or at least the discouragement, of the emergence of superior individualities. Critics of popular government are also inclined to reckon inefficiency, corruption, and selfishness among the inevitable faults of democratic institutions. It is argued that conceptions of duty, patriotism, public service flourish best under some type of authoritarian state and tend to decay, to become weak and flabby in democracies.

The reality of representative institutions is also attacked from many angles. The individual voter is depicted as the helpless victim of the well organized party machine. It is easy for the acute critic with communist or fascist leanings to pick holes in any system of representative government that has yet been devised. If, for instance, the members of the supreme legislative body are selected by voting in individual constituencies, as in Great Britain and America, it can be argued that the popular will is usually falsified because the winning party in an election is apt to receive more seats than its voting strength would warrant. If, on the other hand, proportional representation is employed, as was the case in Germany before Hitler's accession to power, the objection is raised that this leads to a multiplication of parties and increases the difficulty of establishing a working government on a sound and stable basis of parliamentary support.

There is a certain variation, less important, I believe, in practice than in theory, between the two main challenges to liberty at the present time, that of fascism and that of communism. Fascism, so far as one may judge from the public statements of its two chief leaders, Hitler and Mussolini, is committed to the idea of a permanent authoritarian regime, of a government by the élite, with a permanent scrapping of all the features of the liberal state: freedom of speech and press and of political and trade-union organization. A fascist regime is supposed to rest on the will and enthusiasm of a united people; but this combination of will and enthusiasm is a hothouse plant, which is never, apparently, to be voluntarily subjected to the chilling breeze of free criticism.

Communism, on the other hand, might be described, on the basis of Lenin's teachings, as a dictatorship to end dictatorships, a conception that has an ominous similarity to the idea of a war to end war. He sees the "dictatorship of the proletariat" (which in practice has meant the dictatorship of the Communist Party over the Russian people, the proletariat included, and of a small ruling group over the rank-and-file of the Communist Party) as a step forward from "capitalist democracy, which is inevitably narrow, which quietly excludes the poor and is therefore hypocritical and false through and through." As an ultimate stage in human development, when communism will prevail throughout the world, Lenin foresees a society where there is no state authority whatever. The extremely absolute nature of his political philosophy finds expression in his epigram:

"While there is a state there is no freedom. When there is freedom there will be no state."

A mind with a strong predisposition to paradox might accept the theoretical proposition that absolute liberty might emerge from a period of its absolute denial. But it is difficult to discern in the present-day flesh-and-blood experience of the Soviet state any progress toward a society that promises to be either free or classless. The worth of the paper guaranties of the Soviet Constitution has received an expressive commentary in the wholesale executions and arrests of opposition Communists. Not a single one of the normal prerequisites of the regime of advanced democracy so alluringly sketched in the Constitution has been realized. There has been no amnesty for political offenders, no legalization of free discussion of controversial issues within the Communist Party, no permission for the publication of non-Communist opposition newspapers, no authorization for the organization of independent political parties.

So it would seem that fascism and communism, which have so much in common in their criticisms of democratic institutions, are also united in offering a highly authoritarian substitute for the liberal state which is based on political democracy and individual liberty. The sole difference between them is that fascism is more honest in not holding out any prospect of a realization of freedom in any future, near or remote.

Faith in the absolute and permanent value of liberalism, under which term I understand not adherence to any special political party, but belief in the programme of liberty outlined in the first chapter, is being subjected to merciless revision on all sides. It is significant that men of such contrasted views as Mussolini and Professor Harold J. Laski, who stands on the left wing of the British Labor movement, are agreed that liberalism is a transitory and declining political doctrine, which coincided with the rise of the middle class. Disagreement begins, of course, on the question of what is to replace liberalism. Mussolini has a positive answer: fascism. Professor Laski is not quite so sure, but apparently favors some form of communism, somehow divested of the more obviously brutal features of the Russian experiment.

When all the counts in the case against liberty are summed up, the total seems formidable, especially as there is some element of truth in almost all the charges which have been made against the liberal state. There is a tendency in an individualist democracy, where the powers of church and throne and aristocracy, so far as they ever existed, have been broken, to lapse into a vulgar chase after wealth. It may be doubted whether corruption is more characteristic of democracies than of dictatorships; cases of public dishonesty are less likely to be hushed up under the former system. But universal suffrage has its possible abuses as well as its benefits. One of the most obvious of these abuses has received the expressive American term of logrolling; it is the tendency to employ voting power to obtain sectional, local, class, and group advantages, with complete disregard for the larger national interests which may be adversely affected by the process.

Democracies have fallen in the past because their morale became soft and flabby, because they failed to arouse in the mass of their citizens an adequate sense of public spirit. Exaltation of smug mediocrity, especially in periods of great material prosperity, is a cultural threat in a democracy.

The genuine liberal can accept these and other criticisms of the workings of free institutions without admitting for a moment the claim of the collectivist dictatorship that it offers the prospect of a better social order. For the liberal's claims for the type of regime which he prefers are pitched in a much lower key than those of the communist or the fascist.

He does not maintain that the perfect state has been achieved; he may have his doubts whether it ever will be achieved. He thinks not in absolute but in relative terms. And on this principle of relativity, which seems to have as much application in politics and economics as in physics, he is convinced of the tremendous pragmatic value of liberty. He believes, not as a matter of dogma, but on a basis of demonstrable facts and figures, that the method of liberty, where it has been honestly tried, with all the inevitable failings and imperfections, has yielded vastly better results, in terms of material welfare, cultural freedom and progress, and safeguarding of the individual against conscription of the body and straitjacketing of the mind, than the method of dictatorship.

Examined in the light of the principle of relativity, *i.e.* of comparison with other methods of government, the case against liberty loses much of its impressiveness. Consider first the common communist-fascist characterization of democracy as nothing but a sham, a veiled dictatorship of capitalists.

That wealth in an individualist economic order connotes power, that it increases the possibility of influencing public opinion, cannot be denied. But to derive from this premise the conclusion that a democratic state which respects freedom of speech, press, and election is in reality nothing but a dictatorship of the wealthy class is scarcely possible after Stalin, Mussolini, and Hitler have shown how the thorough-going modern dictatorship functions.

The power that wealth confers under a democracy is a very mild and tame thing compared with the absolute authority that is invested in the ruling class in a collectivist dictatorship. To denounce bankers and munition makers in speech or print in America is to commend oneself for public office or for a place in the best-seller lists. To whisper a critical word about a communist dictator in Russia or a fascist dictator in Germany or Italy is an excellent start on the road to a concentration camp.

It is an elementary principle of dictatorship that even minor administrative offices should be filled only by reliable supporters of the ruling party. The Presidency of the United States could not accurately be described as a minor office. Its power and prestige are very great. If the theory that political democracy, under an individualist economic system, is inevitably perverted into a capitalist dictatorship were correct, one would expect the "capitalist dictators" to make sure that the Presidency, at least, if not all minor executive posts, should be held by a man who could be relied on to carry out their wishes. Yet a straw vote, taken among the hundred or thousand wealthiest men in America, would scarcely have shown a majority for Woodrow Wilson in 1916, or for Franklin D. Roosevelt in 1936. Neither is it plausible that British capitalists, in the majority, would have favored the Labor Cabinets of 1924 and 1929 or that French capitalists would have selected Léon Blum as their candidate for Premier.

The theory that the capitalists can manipulate elections and control the entire course of political life through ownership of the leading newspapers, subsidies to political parties, and other forms of financial pressure also does not stand up before any serious factual examination. The money power, for instance, did not prevent the German Social Democrats from building up a very large and well organized press. And this press, on the other hand, did not save them from political extinction when Hitler, with much weaker newspaper support until he came into power, swept the country by other means of mass propaganda. A weak press has not prevented the Labor Party from making a strong showing in British politics. Possession of two of the best edited and most widely read newspapers in pre-Hitler Germany, the "Berliner Tageblatt" and the "Vossische Zeitung" did not make the German Democratic Party a strong force in German political life.

It might be theoretically possible, in a perfectly organized state, to insure a fairer and fuller presentation of minority viewpoints than one finds in democratic countries at the present time. Yet at least one small minority in America and Great Britain, the Communists, seems to compass an amount of written

and spoken propaganda that is out of all relation to
its numerical strength, as indicated at the polls.
And it is difficult to see how anyone with the least
sense of proportion can profess to see no difference
between the official kept presses of the communist
and fascist dictatorships and the press of a democratic country, where some editors and publishers are
doubtless influenced by considerations of property
but where anyone who can find a sufficiently large
audience to pay for his printing and paper costs can
write as he pleases.

Other criticisms of democracy, containing perhaps
some degree of validity in themselves, seem strangely
lacking in force and substance when the situation
under the chief alternatives to democracy, communism and fascism, is considered. Human personality, for instance, may sometimes be dwarfed
and standardized under the influence of democracy.
But in the totalitarian states it tends to disappear
altogether; the individual is simply sunk in the collectivist mass that votes, marches, salutes, cheers
with the regularity and precision of an automatic
machine.

In the liberal state personality may be and very
often is the result of the interplay of half a dozen
conflicting forces. Home influence may point in one
direction, school in a second, church in a third; child-
hood beliefs may be shaken, remolded, refortified by
books that are read in a library, by the personal influ-

ence of an iconoclastic college professor, by the first contacts with the working world.

In the collectivist state, on the other hand, every influence within the control of an omnipotent government is mobilized for the purpose of creating a uniform type of personality, disciplined and regimented to the last degree, trained to regard anything "the leader" advocates as right and to change its mind as quickly as the leader may change his. It is easy to imagine the kind of individual that is becoming a standardized product under the collectivist dictatorship; it is a sort of a human gramophone which plays without a hitch whatever tune the official thought-controllers may call.

Some time ago a Russian Young Communist leader named Sten brought down on his head a storm of criticism by voicing the opinion that "every Young Communist must seriously work out all questions by his own experience and thus become convinced of the correctness of the general line of the Party." The official newspaper of the Union of Communist Youth read Sten a severe lecture and informed him that "his formula is at best the formula of a petty-bourgeois revolutionary individualist, not the formula of a Bolshevist. Sten's Young Communist is some sort of critically thinking personality, who has no concern with the collective experience of the Party."

The contemptuous reference to the "critically

thinking personality" is profoundly characteristic of the spirit of all the collectivist dictatorships. Inasmuch as a high percentage of the noteworthy figures in every branch of human thought and activity have displayed a weakness for "critical thinking," the outlook for the quality of personality in the totalitarian state seems very gloomy.

It would be inaccurate to say that Macaulay's fears about the credit and finance policies of democracies have proved altogether without foundation. It is easy to recall unwise and inequitable measures, adopted under the stress of crisis, as a result of the panic pressure of inexperienced electorates.

But here again the law of relativity must be considered. Comparatively reviewed, the financial record of democracy is vastly better than that of dictatorship. Where the creditor has been let down he has been let down much more mildly. It is decidedly not in the countries with free institutions that direct or indirect defaults on state obligations and raising of revenue by means of forced loans have occurred most frequently.

The unprejudiced and unsentimental lists of ratings of foreign bonds furnish plenty of corroborative evidence of this point. The financial standing of Great Britain, Belgium, and Norway, all parliamentary regimes with free and equal suffrage, is vastly better than that of the lands ruled by a self-styled élite, Germany and Italy. As for the Soviet Union, its internal loans are all of a compulsory character, while it has never enjoyed sufficient confidence abroad to float a bond issue on the public market, although it has disposed of a very small number of its securities privately by offering comparatively high rates of interest.

A democratic parliament or congress often falls far short of ideal standards of grasp of public affairs, independence of thought and judgment, freedom from the pressure of petty local group interests and prejudices. In this, of course, it is a pretty faithful reflection of the human faults and weaknesses of the voters who have elected it. But the least admirable democratic assembly makes the impression of a group of sages and philosophers compared with the gatherings of uniformed or ununiformed robots who make up the mock parliaments of the Soviet Union, Germany, and Italy, whose deliberative functions are restricted to organizing ever bigger and better ovations for the "beloved leader" and to ratifying, always unanimously, any law or decree that may be submitted to them. The most commonplace, back-slapping, vote-catching Congressman from Podunk Corner would be likely to prove a genuine tribune of the people in defending the interests of his constituents, by comparison with the hand-picked Communist, Fascist, or Nazi delegate, trained in the most rigorous fashion to feel a sense of responsibility only to his party leadership, not to his nominal electors.

I had the illuminating experience of attending a session of the Soviet Executive Committee, a legislative body consisting of delegates selected from all parts of the country, in December, 1933. During that year Ukraina, the North Caucasus, and other regions of the Soviet Union had undergone one of the worst famines in Russian history as a result of the Government's refusal to adopt adequate relief measures or to permit foreign relief after the peasants' reserves of food had been stripped bare by two successive poor crops and merciless requisitions for the needs of the Army, the cities, and the export trade. I had only recently returned from a trip in Ukraina and the North Caucasus, where I had found overwhelming evidence in the statements not only of the peasants but also of local Soviet officials that there had been widespread loss of life from hunger and related diseases. The Soviet President Kalinin made one curious reference to the famine. He said, referring to a movement in Austria to organize relief:

"Political imposters ask for contributions for the alleged starving of Ukraina. Only degraded disintegrating classes can produce such cynical elements."

And not one delegate from Ukraina, where in village after village I obtained the most detailed, specific information of outright deaths from hunger, sprang up and gave Kalinin the lie direct. Imagine the storm of protest in the freely elected American Congress or British Parliament if any member should be foolish and heartless enough to say that there had been no suffering or privation among the unemployed: a statement that would be not a whit more mendacious than Kalinin's allegation that there had been no famine in Ukraina.

The fact that this wholly avoidable man-made famine took place at all is about the strongest proof of the pragmatic value of free institutions I have ever found. Is it even conceivable that such a catastrophe could occur in a democratically governed country, where opposition newspapers could publish the facts of the situation and opposition members of parliament could ask embarrassing questions and the government which was responsible for the policies leading up to famine would have to face the voters at a free election? Certainly nothing of the kind ever has occurred in a country with free institutions. And, after having visited the famine-ravaged villages of Ukraina and the North Caucasus and heard the stories of survivors and widows and orphans of the utter inhumanity with which the last pitiful reserves of grain and vegetables had been taken away from them by requisitioning parties on orders from the central government, I carried away a strong, not to say passionate, faith in the inherent superiority of free institutions to dictatorship. This faith will be shaken when and only when a democratically elected and controlled government inflicts on any part of its citizens death and misery on a scale comparable with what the peasants of Ukraina and the North Caucasus suffered in 1932 and 1933.

The liberal does not have to set his claims for the achievements of democracy and individual liberty very high in order to feel a definite margin of superiority over the past, present, and prospective achievements of the dictatorships. If the mistakes, weaknesses, and failures of free governments had been ten times as great as they actually are, liberty should still be prized and cherished—if only for the communist and fascist alternatives with which it is confronted.

Chapter VII

SOCIALISM: A ROAD TO FREEDOM AND PLENTY?

Democracy and individual liberty have hitherto been associated with an individualist, or capitalist economic system. Besides the practical existing alternatives to liberalism there is a theoretical alternative: democratic socialism.

A typical socialist critique of the liberal position might be summed up as follows. Political democracy can only be real and permanent if it is supplemented by economic democracy, *i.e.* by the transfer of the basic means of production, big industries, banks, mines, railways, natural resources, etc., from private to public ownership. Capitalism, with its competitive struggle for international markets and its frequent crises, is historically predestined to lead to war or to fascism, or to both. Consequently socialism is the sole road to freedom and plenty, the sole means of conserving what is best in the liberal tradition.

The attitude of the socialist in the democratic countries of Western Europe and America toward Soviet communism varies from whole-hearted sympathy to downright repudiation of many aspects of Soviet theory and practice. There is, however, fairly general agreement among Western socialists that many negative features of the Soviet system can be attributed to Russia's pre-war tradition of autocracy and industrial backwardness, that socialism would function with more efficiency and fewer executions in a Western country.

The outstanding theorist of socialism is Karl Marx. The social and economic philosophy which he expounded in the monumental "Capital" and in his many shorter works has all the authority of unquestioned dogma in the Soviet Union. The socialist approaches the gospel of Marx with a slightly more critical attitude than that of the communist, whose mentality is essentially fundamentalist. But almost all socialists attach great importance to Marx's ideas and accept his basic principles: that the working class is systematically exploited and defrauded by the employing class, that there is an irreconcilable and irrepressible class struggle between labor and capital, that capitalism, a progressive force when it was overcoming feudalism and unloosing the productive forces of the industrial system, tends in the later phases of its development to become reactionary and must be superseded in time by the higher form of socialism.

Now Marx's entire system of thought is strongly influenced by Hegelian philosophy, with its conception of history as a process of struggle and change,

with synthesis proceeding from the clash of thesis
and antithesis and the progressive force of one stage
of human development becoming reactionary in the
next stage. Believing, in his own words, that "the
mode of production of material life determines the
social, political and intellectual process of life in
general," Marx envisaged history as a series of successive stages of human development, each form of
production being inevitably supplanted, after a
process of struggle, by a higher one. So capitalism,
after overcoming feudalism, must in turn make way
for socialism. The following famous passage in
"Capital" is worth quoting in full, because it shows
how Marx foresaw the doom of capitalism:

> While there is a progressive diminution in the number of
> the capitalist magnates, there occurs a corresponding in-
> crease in the mass of poverty, oppression, enslavement, de-
> generation and exploitation. But at the same time there is
> a steady intensification of the wrath of the working class—
> a class which grows ever more numerous, and is disciplined,
> unified and organized by the very mechanism of the cap-
> italist method of production. Capitalist monopoly becomes
> a fetter upon the method of production which has flourished
> with it and under it. The centralization of the means of
> production and the socialization of labor reach a point where
> they prove incompatible with their capitalist husk. This
> bursts asunder. The knell of capitalist private property
> sounds. The expropriators are expropriated.

Both the symmetry of Marx's philosophical conception of capitalism running its appointed course

and, in its final agony, making place for the supposedly higher social form, socialism, and the rhetoric in which he formulates this theory are impressive and have doubtless won him many converts. There is, however, one fundamental defect in this idea of capitalism withdrawing, or being pushed off the stage of historical development after it has fulfilled its function. (In another work, "The Critique of Political Economy," Marx clarifies further his theory that socialism can only come after capitalism has reached the limit of its productive possibilities, writing: "No form of society declines before it has developed all the forces of production in accordance with its own stage of development.")

The defect is that the theory simply does not square with the plain facts of historical development. The three countries where capitalism has reached its highest stage of development and where conditions are ripest, according to Marx's theory, for transition to socialism, are Great Britain, the United States, and Germany. Not one of these lands seems to be within remote hailing distance of Marxian socialism, with wholesale "expropriation of the expropriators," *i.e.* confiscation of private property in means of production for the benefit of the state.

Great Britain has a powerful Labor Party, which has been in office twice and may be in office again. But the majority of its trade-union members, as distinguished from some of its left-wing intellectuals, seem committed to a programme of gradual, moderate reform, which can be achieved without any violent overthrow of the existing order. Neither socialism nor communism has gained any serious numerical following in the United States.[1]

Germany is perhaps the most discouraging example of all for believers in the Marxian theory that socialism will be realized when capitalism has reached its final, insoluble crisis. The capitalist system in Germany was highly developed. The manual working class, the "proletariat," which Marx regarded as destined by history to lead the socialist revolution, was numerous, well educated, highly organized politically and industrially and steeped in Marxist ideas. The loss of the war and Germany's subsequent economic and financial distress furnished unmistakable revolutionary impetus. But what developed from this potentially revolutionary situation? An obscure house painter, with no prestige, no organized following, no previous propaganda for his ideas, swept the country, smashed to pieces both the Communist and the Social Democratic wing of German Marxism and drove the remnants of these once powerful parties so far underground that within

[1] In the course of a trip in Russia I once met a local Communist Party official in the town of Krasnodar. On learning that I was an American he gave me a glum stare and lapsed into a moody silence. After a few minutes he gave the following explanation of his displeasure: "Marx said the proletariat should take power first in the most advanced industrial countries. America is much more advanced than we are. What's the matter with your American proletariat? Why didn't it act as Marx said it should?"

a few years the younger generation in Germany will scarcely know they existed.

Marx's theory that a long, thorough process of capitalist development sets the stage for the coming of socialism is refuted by the victories, as well as by the defeats of revolutionary socialism since the War. For these victories were won in countries which no orthodox Marxist regarded as economically ripe for socialism, in Russia, where capitalism had only begun to run its course,[2] in backward peasant regions of China where capitalism, in the proper sense of the term, has never existed, in Spain, a land that has certainly not reached an advanced stage of capitalist development.

In sharp contradiction to Marxian theory, actual experience shows that the capitalist system becomes more difficult to uproot, the longer it endures. It is easiest to overthrow in its early stages, when conditions are hardest for the workers. Marx's false conclusion was based on an equally false assumption, that "poverty, oppression, enslavement, degeneration and exploitation" would increase as wealth became concentrated in fewer hands. Precisely the reverse has occurred. The definition of the proletariat

[2] There is an abundance of documentary evidence to show that during the first years of the Bolshevik Revolution Lenin and his leading associates were convinced that socialism could be realized in Russia only if the Russian Revolution were followed by successful proletarian revolts in at least some of the more advanced industrial European countries. In this connection cf. Leon Trotzky, "The History of the Russian Revolution," Vol. III, Appendix II. Stalin's theory of building up socialism in one country was a later improvisation.

as a class "with nothing to lose but its chains" was far more accurate in 1848, when Marx and Engels published the Communist Manifesto, than it is to-day.

Take the case of England, the country where Marx spent most of his adult life and studied working-class conditions most closely. Would any serious student of social history, however strong his theoretical socialist sympathies, support the proposition that the British working class is more impoverished, more oppressed, more exploited than it was in the sixties and eighties of the last century, when Marx was turning out the ponderous volumes of "Capital"? On the contrary, the British worker is better fed, better clothed, better housed and has a far larger share of opportunity and of the amenities of life than he had when Marx was working out his theory of increasing misery and exploitation, leading up to inevitable ultimate socialist revolution.

Marx's system of thought, derived from a blend of Hegelian philosophy, the gloomier wage theories of such classical British economists as Ricardo, Malthus, and Adam Smith, and factual material relating to the grim early period of modern industrialism, did not envisage the possibility of the peaceful transformation of British society which is reflected in occasional Labor Cabinets and in the creation of Labor peers. It took no adequate account of the ameliorating effect on the capitalist system of trade-unionism and coöperation or of the possibilities of labor welfare legislation. Foreseeing a future where a diminishing minority of the financial magnates would grow richer, while the proletarianized masses would grow poorer, Marx did not gauge the cushioning effect on class struggle of the intermediate class between capital and labor which increases in numbers as capitalism reaches a more advanced stage of development. Such a class includes the host of engineers, technicians, salesmen, big and small executives which is needed to man the enterprises of a highly developed modern capitalist system.

The farmer or peasant represents another important element in the population which, so far as experience indicates, cannot be won for socialism. The Russian Communists never won the sympathy of the peasants for their programme of state controlled collectivist agriculture. What they did was to ride into power by exploiting the peasants' desire to seize, for their own possession, the large estates of the landlords, and then to clamp down such a ruthless dictatorship that the peasants, however much they might squirm and writhe, could never obtain the right to own and farm the land on the individual basis which they desired.[3]

Now the divergence between Marxian theory and the realities of social development has an important

[3] The best proof of the peasants' individualist preference lies in the fact that less than 2 per cent of them entered collective farms until extreme state pressure was used to compel them to do so, beginning in 1929.

bearing on the prospects of realizing socialism by democratic means. If Marx's forecast of increasing misery for the large majority contrasted with increasing wealth for the small minority under capitalism had been fulfilled, the coming of socialism would be almost fatalistically predestined. And dogmatic socialists who endow Marx with the omniscience which medieval schoolmen attributed to Aristotle and who are unwilling to examine the prophecies of "Capital" in the light of the demonstrable facts of modern everyday life sometimes look forward to the coming of socialism with the quiet certainty which a certain type of devout believer displays in relation to the millennium.

But the tree of capitalism, instead of decaying until it is ready for the axe of socialist revolution, in accordance with Marx's formula, tends to put forth deeper and tougher roots. The number of people who, consciously or unconsciously, have a vested interest in averting any violent smashup of the existing economic and financial order is certainly greater than it was a century ago, when the capitalist system was in an early stage of development. Individual as well as national wealth has increased; ownership of government securities and industrial stocks is more widely diffused; large numbers of people would be adversely affected if the security of savings-bank deposits and life insurance policies were called into question.

Now, in view of the existing diffusion of property interests, it would be impossible to achieve socialism in the Marxian sense, *i.e.* expropriation of private property in means of production, without treading very hard on the toes of a multitude of small proprietors and investors. And, human nature being what it is, it is unlikely that large numbers of people would see themselves, according to their interpretation of the situation, being robbed without offering some kind of resistance, which, under the circumstances, would mean the beginning of civil war and the end of democracy.

Even if this factor of extra-constitutional resistance did not arise, any attempt to implement a far-reaching programme of confiscation and nationalization would inevitably provoke a tremendous industrial and financial panic. Whatever may be the ultimate theoretical possibilities of a socialist system in the field of production and distribution, it is hard to see how a sharp worsening of the material position of the majority of the people, especially of the wage and salary earners who are dependent for their living on the smooth functioning of a money economy, could be avoided. The average voter is inclined to take the short rather than the long view, to judge by the immediate results of the present, rather than by the theoretical possibilities of the future. Symptomatic of this psychology was the stampede of the British electorate to conservatism in 1931, when it was believed that the purchasing power of the pound was threatened by the half-hearted measures of the Labor Government in meeting the financial crisis. And this crisis was mild indeed compared with the upheaval that might reasonably be expected if a party pledged to a programme of thoroughgoing socialism came into power. So the probable sequel to a serious effort to put such a programme into practice would be overwhelming repudiation at the next election, assuming that democratic methods were preserved. The party in power would see itself compelled by force of circumstances to choose between democracy and socialism, to abandon or water down its full-blooded socialist programme or to set up a dictatorship.

Germany and Italy have proved that, given a favorable set of circumstances, fascism is a working possibility. Russia has proved the same thing about communism, or dictatorial socialism, although the entire trend of events outside of Russia seems to indicate that communism is feasible only for a poor country in an early stage of capitalist development. The remarkably changed tone and emphasis of communist propaganda outside of Russia during recent years seems to reflect a growing awareness of this fact. The French Communist leader Maurice Thorez, for instance, recently made the following very interesting statement:[4]

[4] *Cf.* the "Christian Science Monitor," Sept. 4, 1936.

We are not opposed to private property. . . . We are perfectly in favor of the private ownership of small or even medium-sized farms by the peasants, and of small shops. As to factories, we would not interfere at all with those not employing more than fifty or a hundred workers.

If this statement is sincere it means that the social order at which the French Communists are aiming is something quite different from that of the Soviet Union, where the last small factory owner has long been eliminated and the last remnants of the individual peasants are rapidly being swallowed up in collective farms. It is highly significant, incidentally, that the French Communists, bound as they are to defend the Soviet Union on any issue, do not find it expedient to point to the "triumphs" of collective farming in Russia as an argument to induce the French peasants to abandon their individual ownership for a similar system.

But, while communism (for countries below an undefined minimum level of well-being) and fascism can take the upper hand in periods of abnormal stress and crisis and maintain themselves by means of their well developed technique of terrorism combined with propaganda, socialism, achieved and maintained by democratic means, seems definitely to belong among the world's utopias. By socialism I do not, of course, mean legislation for social reform or individual measures for public, municipal, or cooperative ownership and operation of railways, utilities, markets, factories, and other enterprises. Such measures have been and may be enacted in any democratic state where the majority of the voters are convinced of their expediency.

But socialism in the Marxian sense of "expropriation of the expropriators," of complete abolition of private ownership of means of production is far too violent a change to be brought about peacefully, if past historical experience is any guide. The abolition of slavery in the United States was a minor problem, by comparison, involving far fewer adjustments and sacrifices; yet its solution proved impossible without four years of devastating civil war. Socialism, as I have defined it, is certain to prove, in the beginning at least, a road not to freedom but to dictatorship and counter-dictatorship, to civil war of the fiercest kind.

One sometimes encounters the idea, almost charming in its sheer naïveté, that socialism, in the broad Russian Marxist sense, combined with America's productive capacity would make possible an unprecedented rise in individual earnings and in the general standard of living. The late Mr. Lincoln Steffens on one occasion expressed the opinion that "communism would fit America like a cocked hat" because America had solved the problem of production, while the Soviet Union, under communism, had solved the problem of distribution. The same idea finds still more concrete expression in the following passage in "Russia Day by Day," by Corliss and Margaret Lamont:

> Socialism in America could be depended on to improve things at least as much as has Socialism in Russia. And since America starts far ahead of the Soviet the result in the U.S.A. would be phenomenal. . . . Socialism in America might in rather short order provide every family with the equivalent of a $25,000 annual income.

Putting aside for the moment the highly debatable question of how far socialism in Russia has "improved things," it certainly seems inconceivable that socialism on the Russian Bolshevik model could be introduced in a country with America's historic and economic background without provoking desperate and prolonged resistance. The classes that would have to be "liquidated" would be vastly larger, in proportion to the population. The "kulaks" of Kansas and Iowa and Texas and California, one fancies, would put up a much fiercer resistance when requisitioning and church-closing time came around than the peasants of Russia and Ukraina. And, in the course of the protracted, bitter civil war which would certainly follow any attempt to set up a communist dictatorship in America, the technocratic mirage of a universal $25,000 income would most probably resolve itself into something more like the meagre rations which were doled out to Soviet citizens during the Russian civil war or, more recently, during the years of government-imposed sacrifice for the sake of rapid industrialization, high-speed armament and collectivization of agriculture.

The theoretical case for socialism against capitalism is not exhausted if one admits that it is difficult to envisage a transition to socialism without recourse to violence and at least temporary dictatorship. The convinced socialist may argue that the responsibility for violence will rest with the propertied minority that is obstructing a social change that will benefit the majority. It is also sometimes contended that capitalism inevitably breeds war and that the violence involved in social revolution is both less costly and more purposeful than the wholesale slaughter of modern warfare. Does socialism open up such prospects of improving general material and cultural well-being that it may be considered worth the inevitable price of civil war and subsequent dictatorship?

This price, as one may judge from the experience of Russia and from the more recent developments in Spain, will not be a low one. Civil wars, like wars between nations, tend to become increasingly ferocious and destructive. While the civil war which raged in Russia from 1918 until 1921 took many fewer lives on the battlefield than any corresponding period of the World War it inflicted vastly more casualties from epidemic disease, famine, and the mass shootings and hangings which characterized both the "Red" and the "White" terror.

A similar competition in savagery is going on in Spain at the present time. Here is an indication of the insurgents' military methods, as reported in the London "Times" of August 13, 1936:

A typical example of militarist insurgent tactics to date has been the despatch from headquarters—notably Seville—of detachments, about 100 strong, of Moors or foreign legionaries by motor lorry. On arriving at the outskirts of a dubious village they fire a few rounds from mountain guns, an aeroplane drops some bombs and they then advance. Unless the resistance is too severe they scour the village, shoot all suspected persons and retire to their bases, repeating the process later if necessary.

And here is a counter-exhibit on the government side, as reported in the "Manchester Guardian Weekly" of September 4:[5]

The Committee of Public Health and Safety investigates charges of hostility to the regime, provides safe conducts, organizes search parties for wanted people and shoots them. In five days it shot well over a hundred people in Malaga alone. . . . Some of these people have been killed with shocking violence. One I saw had his head bashed in; another who had not died at the first volley had had his throat cut; others had their fingers, ears or noses sliced off, after death, of course; they are cut off to be taken away as trophies.

The massacres by the insurgents reported in Badajoz and other captured towns seem to be bal-

[5] It is noteworthy, in considering the credibility of this report, that both the "Manchester Guardian" and the correspondent who sent the report have shown definite sympathy with the left-wing Government's cause.

anced by the widespread killings without trial, in
many cases of women, which have been going on
in Madrid, Barcelona, and other cities under the
control of the government. The infamous practice
of holding innocent individuals as hostages, to be
shot in the event of military defeat or of real or
alleged cruelties committed by the other side was
widely adopted by the Soviet regime in Russia. It
has been all too faithfully copied in Spain, where the
number of hostages in Madrid alone has been esti-
mated as high as ten thousand.

To an outside observer it seems certain that civilization will lose, no matter which side may win a
civil war carried on with such barbarity. And the
cruelties of civil war and dictatorship are long-
lived. A vicious circle of terror, bitterness, and desperate attempts at revenge on the part of the individuals and groups subjected to terror and renewed
repression sets in. A dictatorial regime can no more
get on without its occasional orgy of shooting than
a narcotic addict can endure the deprivation of his
drug. It is impossible to condemn whole classes to
"liquidation" and not have a few haunting ghosts.

Quite suggestive in this connection was the case,
reported from the Soviet Union in 1935, of the son
of a liquidated kulak who joined the Union of Communist Youth, concealing his damning parentage,
and deliberately cracked up three airplanes before
he was detected in the sabotage and, of course, sum-

marily shot. This is only an extreme illustration of the bitter, desperate hatred which is inevitably generated by such acts of governmental *Schrecklichkeit* as the "liquidation" of the kulaks, with its accompaniment of women and children and old men dying of starvation and disease. It is a negative factor which must be taken into account in considering the moral preparedness of any dictatorship for war.

Another point that is worth considering in this connection is the significant contrast between the unobtrusive police measures which are considered sufficient to safeguard the life of an American President or a British Premier or the king of a democratic country and the tremendous precautions which are taken to insure every dictator against the bullet or bomb of the potential assassin. After long residence in Moscow I could scarcely believe my eyes when I visited Washington in 1934 and saw people walking directly past the White House without check or hindrance.

Anyone who stopped an automobile because of tire trouble within miles of Stalin's summer villa would be quickly surrounded and cross-questioned by watchful guards. A foreign diplomat whose summer house was about ten miles away from Stalin's villa once remarked to me that he was grateful for the indirect protection he enjoyed, since anyone of suspicious antecedents who appeared in the neighborhood was promptly arrested and eliminated in one way or another. Dictators like to believe that they possess the boundless love and unlimited enthusiasm of the people under their rule. They are conspicuously forethoughted in not giving those of their subjects who may cherish other sentiments any concrete opportunity to express them.

So much for the price in human lives, in freedom, in civilization that must be paid for a socialist dictatorship. What of the compensating fruits?

The material results of the experiment in socialism in the Soviet Union have already been discussed. It has been shown, on the basis of Soviet wage and price figures and crop and livestock statistics that Russia's per capita food balance is less favorable than it was in 1913. The real wages of Soviet workers, two decades after the "exploiting capitalists" have been swept away, are not sufficiently high to tempt any influx of unemployed workers from other countries. One could make a long tour of the Soviet countryside without finding a single collectivized peasant who had been able to acquire a bathtub, an automobile, or a telephone. Are there, however, any inherent advantages in a socialist, as against an individualist, economic system that justify the claim, so often advanced by admirers of the Soviet regime, that, whatever the present may be in Russia, the future is bright, while the "capitalist" world can only look forward to a gloomy cycle of wars and crises?

Some socialist theorists see one such advantage in the correction of the maldistribution of income under capitalism. The extent of this maldistribution, however, tends to shrink when it is subjected to a cold test of facts and figures. The Cleveland Trust Company estimates that an equal redistribution of all wages, all salaries, all bonuses, and all shares of proprietors in 1929 would have yielded an average income of $131 a month. The actual average monthly income earned by all wage workers employed by all manufacturing corporations in 1929 was $119. So a complete "share the income" programme would have only increased the average earnings of the wage worker by about 10 per cent.

But no one except possibly Mr. Bernard Shaw believes that complete equality of income is a practicable ideal. The late Huey P. Long was willing to permit incomes up to one million dollars a year in his "share the wealth" paradise. The Soviet Union today repudiates most emphatically, in theory and in practice, the idea of equal wages and salaries for all. The manager or the chief engineer in a Soviet factory now is likely to receive about ten times as high a salary as the average worker. The spread in income between the skilled and the unskilled categories of labor has also been growing and is deliberately stimulated by the Government.

A good deal of confusion of thought has been caused by calculations that approximately 2 per cent of the American population owns some 65 per cent of the country's wealth. Confusion arises because there is usually no distinction, in the conclusions which are drawn from this statement, between the relatively small share of income that is spent by large owners of corporate property on individual consumption and the vastly larger share that flows back in the form of reinvestment in their own or in other enterprises. The experience of the Soviet Union has conclusively proved that this second and far more important form of abstraction of wealth from the general consumption fund for purposes of new investment is just as necessary under socialism as under capitalism. Indeed, the sacrifices not only of luxuries, but even of comforts and necessaries that have been required of the Russian people for the sake of building new iron and steel works, chemical plants, and electrical power stations could not be paralleled in the recent experience of any Western country.

For a concrete illustration of this point compare the American and Soviet automobile industries. Under an individualist system Mr. Henry Ford has naturally made huge sums of money out of his successful development of the idea of manufacturing a low-priced automobile. But Mr. Ford has used only a negligible part of these profits for his own personal consumption. Enormously the greater part of his earnings has been "plowed back" into the business, making possible the manufacture of more and cheaper cars, or has been utilized for other forms of investment.

What of the comparative position of the Soviet automobile industry? It is managed by a state trust, under the general authority of the Commissariat for Heavy Industry. Like Mr. Ford, the trust engages engineers, executives, workers, and clerks on a wage and salary basis. Again like Mr. Ford, it sells its trucks and automobiles to institutions or individuals at a price high enough to afford a measure of profit. Part of this profit, just as in the case of Mr. Ford, is earmarked for new construction; part of it is taken by the state and is devoted to the promotion of other industries. So far one sees little difference between the private capitalism of Mr. Ford and the state capitalism of the Soviet trust. If one carries the comparison further, however, one finds two appreciable differences: Mr. Ford pays a much higher wage and salary scale and gives his customers a better and cheaper automobile.

The Soviet automobile industry, to be sure, is new and inexperienced, compared with the American. But a trail of incompetence runs through Soviet industrial production in general, especially through the industries which manufacture consumers' goods. The following significant economic information is contained in a despatch from Moscow, published in the "New York Times" of September 24, 1936:

The Soviet Government unsheathed a new weapon today in the fight, so far largely fruitless, to improve the quality of consumer goods, which under socialized production is wretchedly low, while prices are appallingly high, measured either in gold value or in relation to wages. . . . The prices were greatly increased in the cities. Much dissatisfaction is privately expressed by individuals at the fact that a decent pair of shoes now costs 200 to 300 rubles—more than the average monthly industrial wage—and that a poor suit of clothes costs a hundred rubles. A "good" suit, although it would not rank so elsewhere, costs 500.

The theoretical "economy of abundance" under socialism is sometimes approvingly contrasted with the "economy of scarcity" under capitalism. One wonders whether a still harsher epithet might not justly be applied to the economic results of the individualist system if a decent pair of shoes in the United States cost a hundred dollars and a "good" suit two hundred dollars. These would be the equivalents, in terms of monthly earnings, for the prices which prevail in Russia—almost twenty years after the profit-seeking private manufacturer and merchant have disappeared from the economic scene.

Another paragraph in this despatch brings out a concrete example of the extraordinarily low quality of Soviet production. A workers' club bought a hundred and fifty chairs for its clubroom from a state furniture factory. "At the first meeting after the purchase," according to the despatch, "forty-six of the chairs collapsed and most of the others held together only by luck."

The persistently low quality of Soviet industrial production, which has remained unaffected by hundreds of threatening decrees and actual sentences of imprisonment, meted out to managers of the industrial plants which had proved the most flagrant offenders, cannot be satisfactorily explained by references to the relative backwardness of pre-war Russia. Houses in pre-revolutionary Russia were solidly built. The Russian before the Revolution had no reason to expect that a chair which he had just bought would collapse and crash as soon as he sat down in it. The extreme shoddiness of Soviet goods is the result of Soviet conditions: the bureaucratic methods of management which are unavoidable when the state endeavors to manage everything, from steel mills to grocery stores; the high proportion of inexperienced and ill trained executives and engineers in the Soviet industries; the frequent discrepancies between the production plans laid down by central authority and the available stocks of raw material.

Perhaps the most serious weakness which Soviet experience has revealed in a socialist economic order is the complete elimination of the progressive stimulus of competition. The Soviet industrial trust or trading organization is super-monopolistic in character. Private initiative in economic life is entirely

eliminated; and the half-hearted competition which
formerly existed between coöperative and state shops
in the towns has been destroyed with the decision to
supplant the coöperatives entirely with state trade.
Rewards and punishments handed down from above
in arbitrary and haphazard fashion do not adequately
replace the constant impetus to better and cheaper
production and better service to the consumer that
is automatically furnished by a competitive system.
A foreigner who had lived for some time in various
parts of the Soviet Union once observed:

I think three mottoes should be prominently displayed
in every Soviet store. They should read as follows: "The
Public Be Damned." "The Customer Is Always Wrong."
"If You Don't Like Our Store Go Somewhere Else. (Note:
The nearest store is several miles away and probably has no
goods for sale.)"

A vindication of the Soviet system is sometimes
seen in its supposed transformation of the worker
from a "wage-slave" into a proud co-owner of socialist industry. Propaganda can make some people
believe almost anything. Yet it is questionable
whether the Soviet worker, under the present system, feels or can feel any very lively sense of ownership in regard to the factory where he works. He
has no more voice in choosing its manager than a
laborer in one of the mills of the United States
Steel Corporation enjoys in selecting his boss. Like
the aforesaid steel worker he is paid a wage, and

with this his claims on the factory end. He is not entitled to any share in its profits.

If the Soviet worker joins the so-called Stakhanov movement and raises his productivity and output, his wages are raised. So, in due course, is the quota of work required of him and his fellows.[6] This system is not novel or peculiar to socialism. It is known in other countries as piecework, and Karl Marx roundly denounced it in the following terms:[7]

> Piece-wages are very advantageous for the capitalist because they render supervision of the workers almost unnecessary and at the same time offer many opportunities for making deductions from wages, and practising other forms of cheating. On the other hand, this form of wages possesses many big disadvantages for the worker: physical exhaustion as the result of excessive efforts to raise the level of wages, efforts which in fact tend rather to lower wages, increased competition amongst the workers with the resultant weakening of their solidarity . . .

Apparently the piecework method of payment is also very advantageous for Soviet state-capitalism. Sir Walter Citrine, an experienced British labor leader, one of the outstanding figures in the general strike of 1926, after visiting a number of Soviet

[6] The new quotas of work instituted in Soviet industries on July 1, 1936, called for an increase in the amount of work by each worker from 20 to 70 per cent. *Cf.* the "Christian Science Monitor" for August 26.

[7] *Cf.* "Karl Marx," by Franz Mehring, transl. Edward Fitzgerald (New York: Covici, Friede, 1935), p. 392.

factories, made the following probably unpalatable observations to Soviet trade-union leaders: [8]

I said there was more intensive piece-work, bonus systems and general attempts to speed up by hard work than I had ever seen. I was sure that the proportion of piece-work to time-work would bear this out. I said the workers I had seen were working very hard and the women were doing arduous and severe tasks which in a Socialist state were quite unjustifiable.

The Soviet Commissar for Heavy Industry, Mr. Sergo Ordzhonikidze, cast some light on the effect of the Stakhanov movement [9] on those workers who could not stand the pace of speeding up which it involves when he said, in the course of an address at the first congress of Stakhanovite workers:

If a Stakhanovite were to appear there [in the capitalist world] he would be a most unpopular person among the masses of the workers, as such a heightened increase of the productivity of labor would lead to at least one-third and perhaps more of the workers being dismissed, and unemployment would increase. But so fast is Soviet industry expanding, so vast is the Soviet internal market for every kind of product that in Russia workers discharged by one plant are quickly reabsorbed in other work, although not always in the jobs that they like.

The many cases of attacks on Stakhanovites by fellow workers which have been reported in the

---

[8] Cf. "I Search for Truth in Russia," by Sir Walter Citrine (London: George Routledge & Sons, 1936), pp. 129–130.

[9] The name Stakhanovite is derived from the fact that a miner named Aleksei Stakhanov was given credit for initiating the movement.

Soviet press would indicate that it is not only in the capitalist world that the laborer who speeds up his fellows to an extreme degree is "most unpopular." Stakhanovism under state capitalism in the Soviet Union leads to very much the same results as an intensive piecework system of payment under private capitalism. The stronger and more capable workers increase their earnings to some extent by straining their physical efforts to the utmost, perhaps at the expense of their future health. The amount of the increased earnings is limited by the tendency of the employer, whether he be a private owner or a state manager, to raise the quotas of work for a given wage as soon as a number of workers have shown ability to raise their productivity. The weaker workers under this system are pushed to the wall. Their wages are reduced if they cannot stand the accelerated pace; they are dismissed in large numbers as it becomes evident that they are superfluous. And the "jobs they may not like," in Ordzhonikidze's phrase, in the Soviet Union may well be less desirable, as regards real wages and living conditions, than complete unemployment in other countries.

It is a highly debatable assumption that the struggle between labor and capital can be abolished when capital is transferred to the state, when the private owner or manager is replaced by the state manager. For there is an inherent difference of aspiration and

factured goods which they must buy are much higher, in relation to the pre-war price-level, than the prices of the food products which they sell.

As for the workers, the profits paid by the state industries represent one form of "surplus value." A much larger source is represented by the huge turn-over tax on sales of all products, which represents the largest item in the revenue of the Soviet Government. This tax greatly increases the cost of living; it represents a means of transferring money from the pockets of the workers to those of the bureaucrats and the Army. It would be an uncommonly interesting economic study to calculate how much of the value of his production the Soviet worker and peasant is permitted to retain and how much is "extracted" from him for the upkeep of the Army, for the financing of the high construction costs of new military and industrial plants, for the payment of the salaries of a swollen bureaucracy, and for the luxurious motorcars, summer villas and rest homes, and special trains and cars which are part of the perquisites of office for the higher Soviet bureaucracy. One fears, however, that such a study, if honestly made, would never pass the Soviet censorship; it might inspire too many "dangerous thoughts" among the workers and peasants, in the name of whom the Revolution was made.

The most valid criticism that can be made of the individualist, or capitalist, economic system is its inability to organize a rational system of distribution, to insure general full-time employment for labor, technical skill, and industrial plant and equipment. Socialist theoreticians have naturally made the most of this criticism; and Communists like to point to the Soviet Union, where supply of everything, from nails to seats on railway trains, is always conspicuously behind demand, as a country that will never know a sales crisis and that is bound ultimately to overtake the leading capitalist countries in production and in general prosperity.

It is unlikely that an economic system based on private enterprise can ever abolish altogether the alternations of boom and slump, of fat years and lean years which have marked the development of modern capitalism. A free system in economics, like a free system in politics, carries with it, along with many other opportunities, the opportunity to make disastrous mistakes. If investors and speculators, big and small, choose to pay exaggerated inflation prices for land and real estate and stocks in boom periods, there is no practicable means of restraining them, although of course every effort should be made to prevent the obtaining of money on false or fraudulent representations.

A completely stable price level, wage and salary scales that are ideally adjusted in every case to rises and falls in the cost of living are scarcely attainable. Attempts to achieve balance between production and demand encounter a number of formidable obstacles, from the vagaries of weather, which are apt to throw the best laid agricultural plans out of joint, to changes in tastes and habits, sometimes attributable to new scientific inventions.

The best that can reasonably be hoped for is an alleviation of the bad consequences of depressions through such measures as state control of credit with a view to contracting it in prosperous periods and expanding it in periods of slackness, an adequate social security programme and a public works policy which would aim at maximum activity, giving the largest possible measure of employment, in hard times, tapering off to modest dimensions with the passing of the crisis. In the field of agriculture state guaranties of minimum prices to the farmer or peasant producers through large-scale purchase operations and the promotion of freer international exchange of products through a lowering of tariff walls would seem more hopeful means of combating crisis than limitation of production or outright destruction of foodstuffs and raw materials.

A system that cannot assure immunity against crises is obviously imperfect. But in discussing whether socialism is a road to freedom and plenty one must consider not only the defects of the existing economic system, but also the alternative defects of the socialist system, especially those which have been vividly illustrated in the experience of Russia.

One must weigh in the balance the two systems, the individualist and the socialist, as a whole. Because each, along with shortcomings that can be cured as a result of experience and reform, has structural defects that are inherent in the nature of the system.

And when one views in broad perspective the issue between an individualist system that has after all given the masses of the people more in food, clothing, housing, and opportunities for culture and recreation than they have enjoyed under any other, and a socialist system that must list among its "achievements" two major famines, a system of rationing and privation unprecedented in peace time in any other country, that can offer its people near the end of the second decade of its existence goods of phenomenally low quality at inordinately high prices, the answer, to anyone with a sense of relativity, can scarcely be in doubt. Not Russia's somewhat exaggerated pre-war backwardness but the inherent weaknesses of the Soviet economic system, which in all probability would be those of any authoritarian socialist system, are mainly responsible for many of the unfavorable comparisons which any candid observer would have to draw between the living standards of the workers and peasants, to say nothing of other classes in Russia, and those of the corresponding classes in Western Europe and America.

It is always the Soviet Union that is trying to copy and adapt foreign inventions. One never hears of foreign engineers and technical experts going to learn in Russia the superior technique that some theorists associate with socialism. And, no matter how zealously the Soviet Union tries to keep up with the fast pace of scientific and technical progress abroad, the chances are that it will always be left appreciably behind. Universal, all-pervading bureaucratism is not favorable to the adoption of new ideas and methods. A constant atmosphere of political terrorism, where any slip by an engineer or a scientist is likely to be labelled "sabotage," "counter-revolution," or "Trotzkyism" [10] does not conduce to a bold, receptive attitude toward experimentation.

Measured by the important barometer of human standards of living, the high point reached by Soviet socialism is still considerably below the low point touched by the individualist countries in the crisis. If it is a damning reproach for capitalism that it has not been able to distribute properly the plenty it has created, it is a more damning reproach for socialism, in the one country where it has been tried, that it has created no plenty to distribute. The Soviet Union has yet to meet the challenge implied in

---

[10] The following excerpt from a despatch from Moscow in the "Christian Science Monitor" of October 7, 1936, shows how the term "Trotzkyist" is used as a stick to beat anyone who may be out of favor with the existing regime: "A typographical error in a newspaper, a misplaced preposition in another, the serving of spoiled food in a restaurant, an unusual number of accidents in a car-repair shop, such incidents are interpreted as the work of 'Trotzkyists' during the 'heresy hunt' which has followed the Moscow conspiracy trials in all parts of the Soviet Union. . . . Responsible persons are likely to be labelled Trotzkyists for any kind of mistake . . ."

Lord Balfour's statement, in a note addressed to Chicherin, the Soviet Foreign Minister, that Bolshevism, while an excellent means of making rich men poor, was a highly questionable means of making poor men rich.

An American author and critic with pronounced communist sympathies, Mr. Edmund Wilson, recently visited the Soviet Union. He set down his impressions in a number of articles which elicited from orthodox worshippers of Moscow thunders of criticism because of their independence and their admission of those less pleasant aspects of Soviet life which the author had personally witnessed. But one of Mr. Wilson's concluding observations, worth quoting because it represents a fairly general mental attitude among left-wing intellectuals, seems to contain all the elements of a *non sequitur:*

We shall be in no position [he writes] to reprove the Russians till we shall be able to show them an American socialism which is free from the Russian defects.[11]

This is begging the question with a vengeance. It is the new system, rather than the established one, that would seem to be in the position of the challenger, obliged to give some tangible proofs of superiority. Especially is this the case when the new system, as in the case of Russia, during the first fif-

---

[11] Edmund Wilson, "Travels in Two Democracies" (New York: Harcourt, Brace & Co., 1936), p. 321.

teen years of its existence, required the sacrifice of millions of lives and caused tremendous material devastation. The assumption that some kind of socialism is necessary is an indication of the confusion of thought, the loss of all sense of relativity in weighing comparative suffering, which overtook a number of West European and American intellectuals after the crisis. Such an assumption would have been warranted only if the socialist system in Russia had proved its capacity to create more abundance, to distribute it more equitably and to carry out the process with fewer executions and sentences of imprisonment and banishment than the individualist system in, say, England or Denmark requires for its maintenance.

Socialism cannot be a road to plenty because it cannot be a road to freedom. And there is not a single demonstrable exception in any country to the proposition that relative plenty and free institutions are invariably associated. Democratic socialism is a mirage because the changes, dislocations, and sufferings which could not be avoided during the first stage of a transition from individualism to socialism would inevitably cause defeat at the polls if democratic methods were maintained and would very probably plunge the country into civil war.

Authoritarian socialism is simply the most extreme form of the collectivist utopia. Depriving the masses of liberty, of control over their own destiny, it cannot give them real security or material well-being, because it is in the nature of the collectivist dictatorship to sacrifice the individual to the supposed interests of the state, to place grandiose schemes of industrial and military expansion ahead of the everyday comfort and well-being of its subjects.

Finally, a word should be said about the dogmatic assumption that, as capitalism is the cause of war, peace can only be insured by abolishing capitalism. This theory would be more convincing if large-scale wars had never occurred before the coming of the capitalist system. Inasmuch as war was a frequent occurrence both under the slave economy of classical times and under the feudal system, it does not seem to be in any way a peculiar product of the capitalist system.

Moreover, it is precisely the countries where pure capitalism, least affected by state interference, is strongest which are most obviously committed to non-aggressive policies at the present time. One sees far more intensive preparation for war and hears many more martial utterances in Germany, Italy, and the Soviet Union than in America, Great Britain, and France.

There is also little reason to believe that the universal socialist revolution of which Lenin and Trotzky dreamed would usher in an era of peace on earth. If the Soviet Government absolutely dominated every other socialist state, as the Soviet Com-

munist Party today dominates all other parties in the
Communist International, a sort of *Pax Romana*
might be achieved. The same result, of course, could
be achieved if Germany, Great Britain, the United
States, Japan, or any other power achieved a world
empire. But this is a fantastically unreal conception.
No country is strong enough to achieve and maintain
such hegemony. The mere nationalization of factories and natural resources would in no way lessen
the inequality in natural resources which could still
remain a fruitful cause of dispute in an era of socialist states. And it is easy to imagine the doctrinal
wars that might break out if some countries adopted
a Trotzkyist and others a Stalinite brand of communism.

Chapter VIII

THE CHOICE BEFORE CIVILIZATION

Mr. John Strachey, one of the ablest modern communist theoreticians, sees the world confronted by two alternatives: communism and barbarism. Were this diagnosis correct, the outlook for civilization would be dark indeed. A choice between communism and barbarism, a term which Mr. Strachey regards as identical with fascism, is no choice at all.

For everything barbarous that is associated with fascism can be duplicated, and often surpassed under communism. Call the dreary roll of fascist atrocities and name one that is not part of the stock-in-trade of the communist dictatorship in the Soviet Union. Killings of political opponents, wholesale consignment of "counter-revolutionaries" to concentration camps, extension of the number of offenses for which the death penalty is inflicted, punishment of innocent individuals for the offenses of relatives and friends, complete repression of freedom of press, speech, and assembly, regimentation of art and culture to serve the purposes of the ruling party: what item in this list is not just as characteristic of the

Soviet Union as of Germany and Italy? And, if the race fanaticism which is peculiar to the German brand of fascism cannot be charged against the Soviet Union, the class fanaticism which prevails there has taken far more victims.

Fortunately there is a more real alternative to barbarism than communism. This alternative is liberty. Liberty or barbarism: this is indeed the choice before the civilization of the twentieth century.

The term "barbarism" in this connection requires some qualification. Neither Russia nor Germany nor Italy today can be accurately or reasonably compared with the broken fragments of the Roman Empire in the Dark Ages. There has been no such complete break-up of the elements of civilized life as history records after some sweeping incursions of nomadic barbarians. Under the dictatorships, as under the democracies, children go to school and adults read books and newspapers, visit art galleries, attend concerts.

Yet anyone who has lived for a long time in one of the collectivist dictatorships is likely to feel that some of the most precious aspects of civilization are irretrievably gone. I personally had this feeling very sharply on two occasions, once in Russia and once in Germany. In Russia it was the reaction to the death of some unknown peasant children; in Germany it was the result of an attempt on the life of a well known political leader.

I was visiting the village of Zhuke, near Poltava in Ukraina, in the autumn of 1933, accompanied by the head of the local collective farm and a young agricultural expert, both Communists. They were assiduously guiding me to the houses of local Communists and of those peasants who held the posts of minor bosses in the collective farm. I finally decided to pick out a house at random; my companions showed little enthusiasm at my choice, but entered the whitewashed log cabin with me.

Crouched on a bench by the wall was a girl, perhaps twelve or thirteen years old, who looked dull and listless from undernourishment. Had she a father? Yes, he was working in the fields. A mother? No, the mother had died of hunger during the last winter. Brothers and sisters? Four, all dead of hunger. There was no declamation, no outburst of grief, just a stolid repetition of the story, which I had already heard in dozens of peasant houses in southern and southeastern Russia, of men, women, children dying in uncounted numbers because the Soviet government, believing that the peasants were sabotaging its programme of forced collectivization, had taken away the last reserves of food with its requisitions and then failed to supply any adequate relief when starvation came. That such avoidable human catastrophe could occur, and occur without one word of public protest or even comment in Russia, definitely seemed to me barbarous.

The circumstances of my German reaction were somewhat different. I learned on unimpeachable authority the amazing story of how a former Cabinet Minister, Treviranus, was playing tennis on his private court during the fateful days of the June 30th "purge," how a truckload of "SS men," Hitler's black-uniformed special guards, drove up determined to shoot him on the spot, and how Treviranus made a truly phenomenal escape by climbing over the garden wall, jumping into his automobile, which luckily stood outside, eluding his pursuers, and finally escaping to England when the situation became quieter.

Treviranus was not even a Social Democrat; he was a moderate German nationalist who for some reason was considered objectionable to the Nazi regime. It was decided to "bump him off" with no more ceremony than Scarface Al Capone's "mob" would have shown in getting rid of a competitor in the bootleg business. That such a thing could happen in placid, supremely orderly Berlin seemed not only barbarous but fantastic, grotesque.

I have never lived for any long period of time in Italy. But I can imagine that to many residents of Italy, both Italians and foreigners, the murder of Matteoti must have been the symbol of the death of some values of the mellow old Italian civilization which Mussolini could never replace, no matter how many soldiers he put into uniform, how many automobile roads he built or how fast and punctually the Italian trains ran under his guidance.

Regarded as isolated cases, of course, neither the deaths of the Ukrainian woman and her children nor the attack on Treviranus nor the murder of Matteoti could be regarded as of such transcendent importance. What lent focal, symbolic, universal significance to these individual tragedies was that they are so characteristic of the communist-fascist technique of government.

Collectivist dictatorship in any form means a kind of neo-medievalism in its contempt for the individual personality. It means an end of that respect for reason and for individual conscience that is a feature of a modern civilization with roots in the Renaissance, the Reformation, and the French Revolution. A German editor recently remarked to a foreign visitor:

"We have become a nation of mass meetings, mass theatres, mass celebrations, and mass elections."

This statement is true and is equally applicable to the Soviet Union and to Italy. In the collectivist state the individual is completely submerged in the mass. A trained psychologist could find in each of them a remarkable illustration of the powers of mass hypnotism. Get the average Russian, German, or Italian by himself, and the critical note is apt to be uppermost. But in the mass, fear and carefully stimulated enthusiasm operate much more effectively.

This is why every modern-style dictatorship is so eager to line up the individual in its regimented mass organizations, to make him spend much of his time parading and shouting in unison, to leave as little scope as possible for solitary individual thought and reflection.

The collectivist state means the end of the individual personality. It has no tolerance for reason, if this contradicts the supposedly infallible pronouncements of the "leader"; it grants no right to the individual conscience, if this inspires protests against arbitrary arrests and executions in Russia or against Jew-baiting and militarization in Germany. So both the sincere Christian who feels that under certain circumstances he must obey God rather than man and the sceptical humanist who acknowledges no authority higher than that of his own reason must always be spiritual outlaws under the yoke of the collectivist dictatorship.

This yoke bears down especially hard on the creative artist in every field. The ideal of the humanistic civilization that the author, painter, musician should be the sole judge of the form and content of his work is indignantly and vigorously repudiated in all the collectivist states. The National Socialist Party organ *Völkischer Beobachter*, in its issue of May 21, 1934, served the following uncompromising notice on the German artist to get into uniform and march in step:

So long as there remains in Germany any unpolitical, neutral, liberal or individualistic art, our task is not ended. There must no longer be a single artist who creates otherwise than nationally and with a national purpose. Every artist who withdraws from this preoccupation must be hunted as an enemy of the nation until he gives up his intolerable resistance.

An admirable supplementary exhibit in the compulsory harnessing of art to the service of propaganda is to be found in the following definition of the aim of the Soviet writer, as set down in the constitution of the Soviet Writers' Union: [1]

The creation of works of high artistic significance, saturated with the heroic struggle of the international proletariat, with the grandeur of the victory of socialism, and reflecting the great wisdom and heroism of the Communist Party . . . the creation of artistic works worthy of the great age of socialism.

Imagine how Shakespeare, Goethe, Tolstoy, Molière, or any other universal genius would fit into this artistic strait-jacket. The inevitable result of trying to turn literature, drama, and other forms of art into propaganda ballyhoo for an existing political and economic system is to make works of genuinely "high artistic significance" impossible. For the greatest creative geniuses have usually been neutral in relation to the political nostrums of their age.

---

[1] In the Soviet Union, as in Germany and Italy, all authors, in order to earn their living, must belong to a professional union.

Some fine works have been inspired by protest against injustice and oppression. But the world's artistic heritage would scarcely be the poorer for the elimination of all the histories, poems, novels, and dramas that were deliberately written in glorification of the *status quo* of any period. One of Pushkin's most beautiful poems, his "Message to Siberia," was inspired by the courage and sufferings of the Decabristi, the aristocratic rebels against the autocracy in 1825, who were banished to hard labor in Siberia. It begins:

> Deep in the Siberian mine,
> Keep your patience proud;
> The bitter toil shall not be lost,
> The rebel thought unbowed,

and ends with the glowing lines:

> The heavy-hanging chains will fall,
> The walls will crumble at a word;
> And Freedom greet you in the light
> And brothers give you back your sword.

No doubt there were contemporaries of Pushkin who followed the rule, now prescribed for Soviet authors, of zealously praising the existing order. Court poets probably wrote odes about the "great wisdom and virtue" of Tsar Nicholas I and his chief Ministers. But, while Pushkin's generous praise of the proscribed Decabristi lives, the official eulogistic literature of the time is dead and forgotten; and it is not difficult to foresee that a similar fate will have overtaken the Soviet propaganda literature of the present age a century from now.

No art is safe from the meddling of dictatorships and dictators. Modern styles in architecture in Germany languish under Hitler's frown. The compositions of Dmitry Shostakovitch, one of the most brilliant and internationally well known Soviet composers, have been completely banished from Soviet opera houses and concert halls because, according to reports from Moscow, Stalin attended a performance of Shostakovitch's opera, "Lady Macbeth of Mtzensk County," and expressed an unfavorable judgment on it. This suggests very vividly the appalling results that might follow from the accession to power some day of a dictator who was stone-deaf, or even tone-deaf.

Not content with giving their own artists the alternative of propaganda or silence, the collectivist dictatorships try to twist the creative thinkers of the past into propagandists for their pet theories. One of the most revealing and amusing products of Soviet scholarship is a recent book entitled "Shakespeare: A Marxist Interpretation," by A. A. Smirnov. No one would be more surprised than Shakespeare himself to find the ideas which have been discovered in his work by a Marxist investigator. Shakespeare, according to Mr. Smirnov, was "the humanist ideologist of the bourgeoisie of his time" who exposes "feudal knights and profit-knights of primary accumulation." Iago, in Mr. Smirnov's interpretation, becomes "the predatory cynical philistine merchant of the period of primary accumulation," while "Lear" is a criticism of the feudal aristocratic system. Caliban, for the first time in his life, becomes "a true revolutionary," and Shakespeare's tragedies and comedies are described as "militant revolutionary protests against feudal forms, conceptions, institutions," with their roots in "the revolutionary ideas and moods of the bourgeoisie."

Now under any system fools have written about geniuses. But Mr. Smirnov's brand of dogmatic absurdity is far more frequently encountered under dictatorship than under democracy; one can readily imagine a Nazi Goethe and a Fascist Dante that would be about as far removed from the original as this "Marxist" Shakespeare. And, what is still worse, any freak idea that adroitly flatters the ruling system may be made a compulsory article of faith, not open to criticism.

So it is evident that any spread of collectivist dictatorship, either in its fascist or in its communist form, will mean a further submergence of individual personality and a regimentation of thought and cultural life that is not only impossible, but almost unimaginable under free institutions. Belief that such a spread was inevitable has been general, especially during the darker period of the world crisis.

Yet it seems probable that dictatorship has now reached the limit of its conquests. It is noteworthy that these conquests have hitherto been achieved in lands where democracy was an alien and skin-deep conception of government, in Russia with its background of absolutism and popular ignorance, in Italy, where centuries of foreign misrule, poverty, and illiteracy blighted the effective working of a parliamentary system, in countries of Eastern and Southern Europe which lacked essential prerequisites for the successful functioning of democracy, such as general education, wide diffusion of private property, a sense, developed through centuries of struggle and experiment, of the importance of protecting the individual against the arbitrary violence of the state. Germany was culturally best suited for the introduction of a democratic system. But democracy there labored under the fatal handicap of being regarded as one of the terms of the hated Treaty of Versailles. Germany could no more be converted to a belief in the desirability of democracy by having it associated with all the material distress and psychological humiliation of a lost war than the southern states in America could be persuaded of the advantages of Negro suffrage by the methods which were employed during the Reconstruction era after the Civil War.

So up to the present time democracy has only lost ground that was never very securely held. In Spain, now given over to a devastating civil war which seems bound to lead to dictatorship, the whole nineteenth century was filled with rebellions and civil disturbances. The left-wing parties which were in control of the government at the time of the outbreak of civil war in July, 1936, had themselves rebelled against a conservative government, which possessed a parliamentary majority, in 1934. There was not enough balancing moderate strength in Spain to prevent the extremists of the left and the right from fighting their differences out on the battlefields of civil war, instead of compromising and adjusting them in parliamentary debates.

The position of democracy is obviously vastly stronger in Great Britain, France, and the United States. All these countries have passed through revolutions undertaken to vindicate the right of the people to govern themselves. America and Great Britain have no precedent for army meddling in politics (a frequent cause of the downfall of democratic experiments); and France has developed a tradition of orderly republican government stretching back for sixty-five years. The smaller countries that have preserved free institutions also possess their historic backgrounds of freedom. Switzerland's early emergence as a republic, Holland's heroic struggle against Spanish rule are not without significance for the present day.

While there is of course freer expression of criticism and discontent in the democracies than in the dictatorships, the margin of individual well-being under the contrasted systems is so much in favor of the free countries that they are in little danger of seeing their institutions subverted by rebellion from within. War, of course, is an international menace. But there seems to be at least a fair prospect that the area of a future conflict may be largely confined to the dictatorships. In this case the contrast in standards of living under the two systems will become still greater.

One mildly disquieting symptom is the defeatist attitude toward individual liberty and democratic methods of government that is prevalent in some circles of the left-wing intelligentsia in America and Great Britain. Intellectual advocacy of fascism is still a rarity, although fascism of some kind and not communism would certainly be the result of a breakdown of free institutions in a country with a fairly high material standard of living. But there is a pronounced tendency among some liberals and radicals to create a curious double standard of morals, in judging the Soviet Union and the rest of the world. The standard applied to fascist and democratic regimes is hard and uncompromising. It suggests Jonathan Edwards, hell-fire and damnation of unbaptized infants. In the case of the Soviet Government, however, no act of cruelty is too great to be forgiven, ignored, or praised with faint blame.

To get down to more concrete cases, one will find in liberal and radical journals many harrowing accounts of conditions in German and Italian concentration camps, but never a line of suggestion that the inmates of Soviet concentration camps are far more numerous and no better treated. One will look in vain in such journals for any severely critical comment on Soviet laws which would certainly have been denounced in the most vigorous terms if they had been promulgated by Hitler or Mussolini. Imagine the storm about the inherently barbarous character of fascism if Hitler should duplicate the Soviet law which prescribes death for theft of state property or Mussolini should take over the Soviet piece of legislation condemning to exile in Siberia innocent relatives of citizens who flee from the country without passports. And it is hard to understand by what peculiar logical processes individuals who are rightfully indignant over the execution of Sacco and Vanzetti and the imprisonment of Tom Mooney can simultaneously exalt or even condone a system that has slaughtered thousands of Russians on no more evidence than existed in the case of Sacco and Vanzetti, and has herded hundreds of thousands into concentration camps that are no more desirable places of residence than San Quentin Prison without any more reason than could be adduced for the imprisonment of Mooney.

This double standard of morals may be attributed

partly to a lack of sense of proportion,[2] partly to profound ignorance of actual conditions under Soviet rule.[3] There is also a messianic faith in the redeeming virtues of revolution. This faith is not disturbed by the obvious working out, in Russia at the present time, of what seems to be an unfailing law of historical development: that excesses of revolution lead to reaction just as unfailingly as excesses of reaction bring about revolution. This law has received striking fulfilment in the course of the two greatest social upheavals of modern times, the French and Russian revolutions. It is best depicted, in the case of France, not by any detailed history, but by Anatole France's vivid story, "The Gods Are Athirst." Here one sees revolutionary fanaticism, suffering, exaltation, terror reaching an apex and then, after the Ninth Thermidor and the execution of Robespierre and his leading associates, a new era setting in, milder as regards terror, also less idealistic, with everyone deciding to forget about impossible ideals, enjoy life, and get rich.

[2] Every honest believer in democratic government must have resented the arrest of the Communist candidate for President, Mr. Earl Browder, by the Terre Haute police for the purpose of preventing him from exercising his constitutional right of free speech. But how lucky any anti-Stalinite speaker, Communist or non-Communist, would be in the Soviet Union if he could freely address large audiences in all the large cities of the country with no more serious penalty than a day in the lock-up of some Russian Terre Haute, such as Kursk or Kolomna!

[3] The index of Mr. John Strachey's book "The Nature of the Capitalist Crisis" reveals only one reference to the Soviet Union, a dogmatic statement, unsupported by any concrete evidence, that the dilemma of profits or plenty has been satisfactorily solved there. Such a root-and-branch critic of the capitalist system might, one would think, have profitably devoted a little more attention to the problems and defects which experience has indicated in the alternative communist system which he prefers.

It is just such a Thermidorian stage that is now in progress in Russia. The Soviet bureaucracy is constantly improving its material position by comparison with the "proletariat," the theoretical sovereign of the country. Marriage and frequent childbearing are strongly recommended to the "emancipated" women. Army and navy officers receive old resounding titles instead of the simple "comrade commander" of revolutionary days. The manager in the factory, the parent in the home, the teacher in the school, all are being vigorously strengthened in authority. The dictatorship of the proletariat has never been anything but a play with words, an unreal and unrealizable conception; and now it becomes increasingly clear that the true beneficiary of the Russian Revolution is not the manual working class as a whole, still less the people as a whole, but the military, police, political, and economic bureaucracy that is firmly entrenched in the seats of power. Some of the members of this bureaucracy are ex-workers, and some are not. But none of them will ever work with their hands again so long as the present regime survives.

Revolutionary terrorism, if one may judge from the double experience of France and of the Soviet Union, passes through three stages, reflecting the changing psychology of the transition from the destruction of old inequalities to the consolidation of new ones. First there is mob violence, some of it sporadic and accidental, some it directed against individuals who are personally unpopular. The victims of this stage are mostly members of classes prominently identified with the old regime.

The second stage is that of organized governmental mass terror, motivated partly by the determination to smash counter-revolution, partly by the necessity of suppressing very sternly the disillusionment that naturally makes itself felt among the masses when the revolution brings war and hunger, not the peace and plenty that have been promised.

And finally, when the new revolutionary order has become firmly established, when the new classes that have risen to power on the ruins of the old wish to insure and stabilize their position, a third phase of terror begins. The Revolution, in Taine's brilliant phrase, emulates the crocodile and begins to devour its young. When one sees the names of such prominent old Bolsheviks as Zinoviev and Kamenev, Smirnov and Yevdokimov in the list of sixteen who were shot for alleged conspiracy against Stalin, when such outstanding figures of the first years of the Revolution as Radek, Sokolnikov, Pyatikov, Bukharin, and Rykov are reported as arrested or suspected in connection with similar conspiracies, it is evident that the Thermidorian period of the Russian Bolshevik Revolution is here.

There is no new heaven and new earth at the end of the blood-soaked road of social revolution. There are only new individuals, new groups in power,

shooting down their own more extreme former comrades as a means of keeping themselves there. Under
circumstances of extreme oppression, where no other
means of redress is left, revolution, like war, may be
necessary and justifiable. But revolutions, like wars,
tend to become more destructive with the passing of
time. There is not the slightest justification for re-
sorting to this uncommonly costly means of forcing
political and economic change while the machinery
of free institutions continues to function, most especially as the results of revolutions almost invariably
fall so far short of the dreams of the fanatical idealists
who are in the foreground during their early phases.

Viewed realistically from the standpoint of the
common man, the collectivist utopias do not seem
to deliver the goods. The abolition of normal safeguards of personal liberty, of security against arbitrary arrest and imprisonment opens the way to an
amount of cruelty and injustice that must be seen
to be adequately realized. Mr. Sinclair Lewis's picture of the prospective brutalities of a fascist regime
in America is not in the least overdrawn. And, if the
experience of Russia is any guide, these brutalities
would only be greater, affecting more people, if communists rather than fascists were in supreme power.
It is difficult to estimate the reserves of human besti-
ality and sadism that have been slowly, gradually, imperfectly bridled by the formation of democratic institutions and that immediately reappear in full force

when the bars are let down under a dictatorship.

The causes of class antagonism are not removed in the collectivist states; only the symptoms are driven underground. People do not cease to suffer from poverty and want; they are only obliged to cease complaining. Not one of the present-day dictatorships gives its subjects a standard of living remotely comparable with that of the leading democratic countries.

Much of the inflated prestige of dictatorship, much of the impatient contempt for democracy that one encounters today is attributable to an exaggerated reaction against a misplaced emphasis in nineteenth century thought. Historical development at that time was interpreted too exclusively in political, legal, constitutional terms. Economic influences were apt to be neglected or pushed into the background.

Many political and economic publicists of the present time, I think, have erred in precisely the opposite direction. They have become so obsessed with a purely economic interpretation of history that they overrate the power of wealth and very much underrate the progressive significance of the curbs which the development of free institutions has placed on the arbitrary exercise of governmental power. They are altogether too ready to sacrifice liberty lightly on the altar of some doctrinaire blueprint of the perfect state, drawn up in accordance with fascist or communist specifications.

Now nothing could be more utopian in the worst sense of the word, more impracticable, more foredoomed to failure, than an attempt to solve the problem of wealth without considering the much more important problem of power. For one of the most serious and justified criticisms of large aggregations of wealth is the undue power and influence which they confer on their owners. This is a permanent menace in a democracy, a menace for which constant vigilance and a high sense of public spirit are the sole remedies.

But the power which wealth confers in a country that possesses freedom of speech, press, assembly, and voting is a very mild and tame thing compared with the absolute power that is vested in the rulers of the collectivist dictatorship. It is difficult to see how abuses arising from inequality of wealth will be cured by instituting a form of extreme inequality of power. The very concept of dictatorship implies that some people are dictating and others are being dictated to. In the light of all historical experience, it seems inevitable that the individuals and groups which are at the transitive end of the dictating process will build up not only a privileged status, but also a favored material position.

The idea, implicitly held by communists and uncritical admirers of the Soviet Union, that the remedy for the evils of private capitalism is to make the state the sole capitalist, simultaneously depriving the individual, under one-party dictatorship, of all effective safeguards against exploitation and oppression by the state, deserves more examination than it has received. Many of the most ruthless acts which can be laid to the account of private capitalism are attributable to the bigness and consequent sense of irresponsibility of some private corporations. But what corporation can be bigger, more irresponsible, more "soulless" than a state that operates everything from steel mills to barber shops, that sets the price which the peasant gets for his grain and the wage that is paid to the worker in mine or factory?

Such a state, even though its founders be the most high-minded idealists, is bound to turn into an extreme form of tyranny unless its enormous powers are somehow checked and controlled by counterbalancing forces from below. The most effective means of assuring "government of the people, by the people, for the people" are periodic free elections, with full liberty of speech and press and freedom of trade-union organization. All these checks are eliminated under both fascist and communist brands of collectivist utopia.

Mere reiteration of the principles of civil and political liberty is, of course, no adequate remedy for the maladjustments which have come to society with the machine age. Still less is salvation to be found in scrapping these liberties on the demonstrably illusory theory that economic welfare and security can be bought at the price of freedom.

For liberty is not a bare abstraction, an academic formula. It is a supremely important practical instrument for carrying on the organized life of society with much better material results and vastly less cruelty, oppression, and injustice than one must reckon with under any dictatorship. It should always be associated with progress, never with stagnation and the mere maintenance of the social and economic *status quo*. It will be a bad day for any country when the idea of liberty can be plausibly represented as a screen for wealth and special privilege. So far as there is definite human responsibility for the wasteful ferocity of violent revolution, it must lie mainly at the doors of those die-hard reactionary classes and groups that are too shortsightedly selfish to make the compromises, concessions, and adjustments that are necessary for orderly progress. A common bond of stiff-necked futility links the Roman Senator of the time of Sulla, the French aristocrat of the middle eighteenth century, the conservative Russian landlord or official of pre-war days.

The grip of the modern-style collectivist dictatorships is strong. They seem proof against anything but the unpredictable chances of unsuccessful war. Yet there is a fraudulent element in their claims of universal popular support that crops up again and again. It is a far more convincing achievement to win a 55 or 60 per cent majority in a free and honest election than to receive a unanimous vote of confidence (no other kind has been known for many years) at a Soviet Congress or a 99 per cent majority in a Hitler plebiscite.

John Milton's strong manly English style is old-fashioned. But the thought of the following quotation rings just as fresh and true today, with Western civilization facing the alternatives of democracy or dictatorship, as in Milton's time, when England had been the first large country to repudiate the divine rights of kings: [4]

Certainly then that people must needs be mad or strangely infatuated, that build the chief hope of their common happiness or safety on a single person; who, if he happen to be good, can do no more than another man; if to be bad, hath in his hands to do more evil without check than millions of other men. The happiness of a nation must needs be firmest and certainest in full and free council of their own electing, where no single person, but reason only, sways.

The struggle for liberty is unceasing, although the figures in the struggle change. In Voltaire's time kings and priests could fairly be regarded as outstanding enemies of human freedom. Now they have given place to communist and fascist dictators.

In an age of rapid social change and scientific ad-

[4] Cf. the essay on establishing a free commonwealth in "Areopagitica and Other Prose Works" (Everyman's Library ed.), p. 169.

vance it is certainly wrong to make a dogma and a fetish out of any detail of economic organization. It is not of vital importance whether railways and public utilities and similar enterprises are nationally or municipally or privately owned. Every country, provided it retains democratic self-government, can be depended on to work out the arrangement which is best suited to its needs.

But it is a matter of tremendous importance whether people can speak and write and vote freely, whether they can go to bed without fear of being dragged off to questioning, torture, exile, or execution by some irresponsible secret police, whether they can talk above a whisper about public affairs when there are unknown listeners. Once the juggernaut of collectivist dictatorship rolls over a country, irreparable damage is done to its standards of culture, to the quality of its human relations, to the most elementary canons of common decency. Freedom, once lost in a modern dictatorship, can be regained, if at all, only by a long and incredibly painful struggle. With the record of communism and fascism written large for all to read, the absolute and unconditional value of human liberty is no longer a theoretical or debatable proposition.

Patrick Henry's flaming phrase, liberty or death, is a sober statement of the alternative that confronts civilization in the twentieth century.

INDEX

HETERICK MEMORIAL LIBRARY
335 C44   onuu
Chamberlin, William / Collectivism, a fals

3 5111 00146 1304